MARRIAGE
A PATH TO SANCTITY
2nd Edition

MARRIAGE

A PATH TO SANCTITY

2nd Edition

JAVIER ABAD
EUGENIO FENOY

SINAG-TALA
PUBLISHERS, INC.
Manila

Originally published as *Amor y Matrimonio 2^{nda} Edicion*
© EDICIONES RIALP, S.A.

MARRIAGE, A PATH TO SANCTITY
© 1988 & 2002 English translations
   by Sinag-tala Publishers.
Published 1988. Second Edition 2002
Printed in the Philippines

   This second English edition was published in May
2002 by Sinag-tala Publishers. The publishers wish to
thank Ms. Anna Maria Z. Nisce for the translation
and editing of this second edition.

ISBN: 971 554 153 4

SINAG-TALA PUBLISHERS, INC.
Fax: (632) 8969626
E-mail: stpi@info.com.ph
Website: www.sinagtala.com

Contents

4   FECUND LOVE

5   RESPONSIBLE PARENTHOOD

6   CHASTITY IN MARRIAGE

7   THE SACRAMENT OF MATRIMONY

8   THE SANCTIFICATION OF MATRIMONY

Introduction

We realize now, more than ever, that the family is the primary concern of anyone who cares about the present and the future of the human race. Nevertheless, it seems that the rights of the family are under attack in intellectual and social spheres as well as through certain means of public communication sympathetic to the anti-life politics of advocates for population control. Thus the family unit is continuously assailed; and its primordial rights, morality, economy, and its very role in society, subject to debate. Nonetheless the current moral scenario demands that we take stock of the sacredness of the family. In the face of widespread birth control, abortion and infanticide, the increasing number of marriages contracted through the Internet, the rampant practice of premarital sex which leads to more and more failed marriages, divorces, and marital infidelities, such a reflection must be done with an ounce of daring and insight.[1]

We are talking about a family that is founded on marriage, a natural institution with specific goals and benefits, the primal cell of society whose truth is rooted

---

[1] Cf. Francesco di Felice, Vice Secretary of the Pontifical Council for the Family, *La santa famiglia e il prossimo incontro mondiale delle famiglia a Rio de Janeiro*, Osservatore Romano, 29 December 1996.

in the heart, in human nature and in the experience of all civilizations. This means that the family belongs to the patrimony of mankind. It is a reality that opens itself to all people of all centuries, to believers and non-believers. Our reflection is not confined to what reason can grasp; in a special way, it also takes into account the sacramental dimension of marriage and the abundant wealth that faith has to offer.

Writing to the countries of Latin America, but in a language understood by all, Pope John Paul II acknowledges the urgent need for a widespread catechism of the Christian ideal of conjugal communion and of family life, which includes the spirituality of fatherhood and motherhood. The Pope sees the urgency of paying greater pastoral attention to men's roles as husbands and fathers, as well as to the responsibility they share with their wives in marital and family duties and in the education of the children. One should not overlook the serious preparation young people need before they get married, which is to impart to them clear Catholic doctrine about the theological, spiritual and anthropological aspects of the sacrament of Matrimony.[2]

Getting married is a major event in the life of many. It is an act that is specific to human beings—because only rational beings contract marriage—and an important status in social, ecclesiastical and civil spheres. The family is the foundation of all stable societies. It is indispensable to the common good and, therefore, the most natural and necessary union in a community. Its origin is God, the Author of a person's social condition and, as a consequence, it precedes

[2] Cf. *Ecclesia in America* no. 46.

any other institution: in the order of nature, marriage is the earliest form of association between a man and a woman.

Man is a "relational" being. He can communicate and engage in a dialogue with another. One's personality is formed through one's interaction with other lives, an exchange that ranges from the most superficial and accidental, to the most intimate and profound. Love is the deepest level of communication. Here, one person penetrates the life of another by giving the best one has, which is one's self. A man and a woman need company; they need to be surrounded by people. However, one is not satisfied with chance and transitory meetings, much less with mere physical contact. Man's social dimension requires something deeper and which has more profound repercussions. For many, the bulk of that "something" is marriage. *Therefore a man leaves his father and his mother and cleaves to his wife and they become one flesh.*[3] This is how Sacred Scriptures express the reality of marriage: two beings meet and fall in love with each other and so unite themselves for always in a definitive way, thus forming an inseparable, indissoluble and perpetual union.

When a man and a woman get married they seek in it a new dimension that would perfect their lives. In this giving of one's self, none of the two experiences a loss or a diminishing of one's personality. On the contrary, their lives acquire a broader horizon which opens doors to a positive fulfillment of their social nature. Some might think marriage "ties one down" and so entails the loss of a significant part of one's nature. But it does not go that way. When the spouses

[3] Gen 2:24.

truly give themselves, soul and body, to one other, they place themselves in an ideal situation to abandon their selfish ways and to find in each other the necessary complement that will bring them to discover a fresh and attractive way of life. The spouses enrich each other by a sharing of talents and virtues. They lead this new way of life through a union that gives birth to a distinct being: *And they become one flesh*. A married couple's fruitful love—their mysterious participation in God's creative power—brings forth new lives, making the world a greater and better place to live in. And together, as a family, they help each other, bring the children to discover the joy of living, and radiate joy that makes life pleasant for everyone around them.

Before delving into our subject matter, we must first consider the unique dignity of the family: Sacred in its earthly mission and supernatural in origin, nature and end. God looks at marital love with special fondness because he created it to perpetuate the human race and to make this union of rational beings divine. This is particularly true when the Word became flesh in the womb of a betrothed virgin, Mary most holy, a woman who belonged to a very ordinary family. With marriage elevated to the level of sacrament, no one can doubt the family's transcendent mission. The future of society and of the Church is forged within the family. In it one learns and practices the human and the supernatural virtues, and from it should come society's leaders and vocations to the apostolate. Christ sanctified family homes with the sacrament of Matrimony and he expects these to be the foundation of his redemptive work.

Pope John Paul II often says that the future of humanity takes place in and through the family. It is therefore urgent that all men and women of good will exert the effort to conserve the values of the family and strive to meet its needs. Just as it is useless to expect the body to be strong and healthy when the heart is weak, all efforts to promote a safe and orderly society will be vain as long as the family does not possess inner strength and moral stability. World leaders, local and national leaders, makers of public opinion, and leaders of various community groups commit a real crime against humanity if, instead of promoting family unity, they neglect it or actively demean it.

Unity and harmony in a family means adhering to the inviolable laws of the Creator. In this way, the family is better prepared to observe all other legitimate laws of society. Forsaking the divine commands promptly leads to the disintegration of human and earthly loyalties. Those who build the future of nations should not weaken family ties or worse, favor their dissolution in the name of a poorly understood sense of freedom or citizenship. Rather, society's leaders should provide the conditions for the adequate development of the family by fighting all forms of moral and material penury. In the midst of a society that is insensitive to the fundamental values of love, married couples are called to stand as witnesses to gratuitous love, often hurt by selfishness. They are called to testify to openness to life, now cheapened by unbridled sensuality and pleasure-seeking. They are called to attest to marital fidelity, which has given in to fickleness and frivolous relationships based on pure instinct.

To understand how it is to live in a real home, Christians—and even non-Christians who understand genuine human values—do well by turning their eyes to the Holy Family. Nazareth reminds us of what a family is: a communion of love, a life of simple and austere beauty, and a union that is sacred and inviolable. The Holy Family teaches us the family's natural role in society and makes us see that education within the family is sweet and irreplaceable. Contemplating the model of the home wanted by God—which is a natural institution—we break away from the brash and superficial idea of marriage and the family as mere man-made institutions or products of the times. The marital union suffers from a series of eroding values that offer no stability but instead weaken the family by placing a high premium on excess and dissipation.[4]

Truly Christian spouses know how to identify and fight the many enemies of the true good. These enemies are not just individualism, hedonism and pragmatism, but also skepticism, a shrunken moral and social conscience, the absence of ideals, and the lack of sound discernment when it comes to judging the moral and material misery around us. The success of a family is measured above all by the exercise of total love, which is the fount of unity. Such a love demands continuous mastery over one's ego. A family that wishes to be healed must begin by rediscovering love and its demands which can never be shunned. And for no mean reason. We are reckoning with an institution that the Creator has wisely brought about to fulfill his plan to save man.

---

[4] Cf. Cardinal Alfonso López Trujillo, Pontifical Council for the Family. *The Family: Gift and Commitment, the Hope of Humanity.*

Love cannot be a mere instinct or an empty senti-ment: its origin is divine. Moreover, it is a participation in God's love and therefore must transform itself into a true and noble offering. Thus understood, love enlightens the mind, strengthens the will and enkindles the heart, to the point of edifying man, preserving him against all forms of degradation. Such love, when properly valued and turned into virtue, is linked with generous self-sacrifice, no matter how difficult, and offered to God for the good of the home and, conse-quently, of society. It is a love that strengthens and restores warmth to symptoms of weakness or indif-ference which nowadays arise so frequently, seriously damaging communities and organizations. God desires human love in all its forms, manifestations, meanings and implications. He wishes marital love to be directed toward the ends that he established, working together with the sacramental life. Thus marital love remains fresh and enduring, solid against the threats of routine and the uncertainties in life.

As John Paul II puts it: "The inner principle of that task, its permanent power and its final goal is love: without love the family is not a community of persons and, in the same way, *without love, the family cannot live, grow and protect itself as a community of persons.*"[5]

Talking about the family of Nazareth, Mary's and Joseph's choice to remain virgins is not the only norm. Nevertheless, we can consider theirs as an example of docility to the divine plan. For God's design also embraces fecundity, the zealous respect for life (even if

---

[5] *Familiaris consortio* 18.

the womb remains barren), the chastity of the spouses, the unity and indissolubility of the marital bond, the education of the children, and a sense of responsibility for one's dignity and that of the other.

The values that are more proper to a wife and mother are incomparably synthesized in Mary. She is the standard by which any woman can evaluate and actualize her true greatness. On the other hand, the man's acknowledgment of his wife's marvelous mission in the light of the Gospel is authentically personified in St Joseph. St Joseph encountered difficulties in obeying God's instructions but he learned to understand Mary's mission and accepted the divine appointment to remain by her side. Likewise, the husband should esteem his wife's vocation and wisely collaborate with her so that she may understand it better, appreciate it more deeply, and never feel burdened by it.

The Old Testament tells us of families like Noah's and Abraham's, from whom many blessings flowed unto generations of men. The Redeemer sprung from the line of David. The Son of God himself formed an earthly home with Mary, his Mother and, by divine design, Joseph, his foster father. Many of Jesus' teachings are inspired by events in the home. The apostles were called within a family setup. Peter and James each found the Master through their brothers, Andrew and John. The New Testament mentions people who, after an encounter with Jesus and his doctrine, ended up converting their whole family: Mary, Martha and Lazarus; Zaccheus, whose conversion brought salvation to all his house; Alexander and Rufus, the sons of Simon of Cyrene, who carried the Lord's Cross. The first Christian communities arose from the families of

Mark, Timothy, and Aquila and Priscilla. "Families who lived in union with Christ and who made him known to others. Small Christian communities which were centers for the spreading of the Gospel and its message. Families no different from other families of those times, but living with a new spirit, which spread to all those who were in contact with them. This is what the first Christians were, and this is what we have to be: sowers of peace and joy, the peace and joy that Jesus has brought to us."[6] The Apostle Paul's counsel further sustains us: *Put on then, as God's chosen ones, holy and beloved, compassion, kindness, lowliness, meekness, and patience, forbearing one another and, if one has a complaint against another, forgiving each other; as the Lord has forgiven you...And above all these put on love, which binds everything together in perfect harmony.*[7]

Matrimony as a divine institution aimed for the good of the spouses and of society may be considered from a rich human standpoint and from its abundant supernatural implications. We shall reflect on this in the succeeding chapters, with quotations from a good number of authors. More than trying to be original, we wish to organize into a coherent body those basic elements that make up the life and the well-being of many. We wish to identify the ideal environment wherein one can wage this battle of love and friendship, as well as seek earthly happiness and prepare one's self for the life hereafter. Which is what human life is all about. We trust that our frequent reference to other authors— all authorities and experts in their fields—would not

---

[6] St J. Escrivá, *Christ is Passing By*, Sinag-tala, no. 30.
[7] Col 3:12-14.

make your reading difficult. Rather, we hope to impart clear ideas and help you draw some benefit from this effort.

We appreciate the stimulating response and feedback from many married couples who, after having read previous editions of this book, attest to having saved or strengthened their marriage by God's grace and their personal effort. They remain happy couples, though perhaps, in the eyes of the world, not as happy as they should be. Nevertheless they are working it out and winning in the eyes of God, who helps them with his love and with the spiritual strength that the sacrament of Matrimony has to offer. The experiences, comments and observations of these couples have been very useful in coming up with this updated and expanded edition which takes into account the new circumstances and factors that marriage and the family have to reckon with in this third millennium.

To all, our warmest thanks.

1

The Period of Courtship

> *Getting married means giving half your soul to your spouse and receiving the other's half in return. If both halves complement each other, what heaven it shall be! But if they do not, what hell shall be suffered! For whereas before we had two complete lives, now we have two broken and shattered halves. Let those in love therefore take careful stock of the soul they surrender as well as of the soul surrendered to them.*
>
> (Severo Catalina)

Courtship is a stage in the process wherein two people decide to get married. Call it the period midway being a "swinging single" and a married person. A period that is neither indefinite nor permanent because courtship, in itself, is not an end but a means to prepare two people in the best way possible to start a life together. It is during this stage that a man and a woman, who initially like each other, try to get better acquainted. Love can blossom from this mutual knowledge and the two can decide if they are meant for each other and if they can start walking the same path together. At this point in their life, the steady dating couple establishes a commitment of sorts from which one or both can back out, since this commitment is neither final nor indissoluble. One can always walk out the back door, so to speak, in case one's current girl or boyfriend is not yet the "right one." Nevertheless, the commitment made during courtship requires the virtues proper to any serious relationship between two mature persons. *Loyalty* demands that one should desist playing the field. *Respect* for each other's intimacy in body and spirit guarantees that two people in love preserve for each other the best of themselves, like a brand-new gift bearing a warranty seal, for their future union as husband and wife. The period of courtship also requires the couple to exert the *effort* to gradually raise the quality of their love, advancing from the sentimental, unstable, selfish and irresponsible stage to a mature love that leads to generous self-giving, which is characteristic of married life.

This gradual process requires that the two get to know each other from the *inside*, that is, down to the deeper aspects of personality, tastes, ideals, and values, to see whether or not they are compatible with each other. Knowing one leads to loving one.[1] And the period of courtship is a time for a man and a woman to get well acquainted, with a view to a lifelong partnership. Because each one is a complete being who must learn to be sufficiently detached from one's self in order to be fully integrated with the other: if what one gives

_____

[1] Cf. Gerardo Castillo, *The Mad Rush for Life*, EUNSA, Madrid.

does not harmonize as best as possible with what one receives, then the end result is failure and disillusionment. It is not a question of trying to have identical or uniform personalities, but rather of complementing each other well.

There is a joke that goes, "The first years of marriage are like trying on a new pair of shoes. Don't expect a perfect fit." Courtship is the time to know whether or not the couple "perfectly fit" each other. It takes mutual adaptation to achieve such harmony; and adaptation entails knowing what there is to adapt to. Harmony must be achieved at courtship stage, otherwise, very difficult marital problems will surface afterwards; and when they do, the couple will feel short-changed. A nagging sense of failure will creep in, jeopardizing their happiness and that of their children.

People in love should live their courtship in a spirit of freedom. They must be open and sincere with one another and always strive for mutual understanding, knowing how to express their affection in a chaste and dignified way, humbly and assiduously seeking the guidance they need to take on this challenge with responsibility. For this, the couple practice a body of virtues which, if well exercised, will make their courtship a joyful discovery, a perfect initiation to marriage. The preparation for conjugal and family life then becomes a privileged period wherein God poses to the couple the question of a vocation to the married life. The decision then cannot be hasty or left to chance because the matrimonial union is of immense value, first, to the spouses, and then to the entire community.

There was a time when society advocated such preparation because it recognized the values and benefits of the marriage bond; separation and divorce were rare then and were generally considered a social plague. Nowadays, however, society contributes to the marked break down of the family and to the under-mining of the conjugal commitment. The rate of marriages, for one, has dropped in many countries especially among the developed nations. People marry late and, as a parallel, the rate of divorce and separa-tions increase even among those who have just started a life together. Thus, the nagging question: Are those who get married really prepared for it? Preparing to receive the sacrament and to lead a life together proves to be a great need for the well-being of the spouses and of society itself. Consequently, there is a growth in interest and initiative to find suitable answers. Questions about the family crop up in the minds of would-be spouses, inviting them to understand the meaning of responsible and mature love in the community of life and love which they will call their family.

Matrimony therefore presupposes a response to a vocation and an acceptance of the mission to be a sign of God's love to all men, a participation in Christ's definitive marriage with his Church. The spouses cooperate with the Creator and Savior in the gift of love and life and their preparation can be considered an adventure of faith that does not end at the altar but goes on in a permanent way to life in a family setting. The experience of many married couples, parents and educators shows that the period of courtship is not only one of mutual discovery but also of a deepening in the faith and, as a consequence, a deepening in the supernatural gifts that foster personal and interpersonal spirituality.[2]

CHASTITY AND GOING STEADY

> *Courtship should be a time for growing in affection and for getting better acquainted. As in every school of love, it should be inspired not by a desire of getting, but by a spirit of giving, understanding, respect, and kindness.*
>
> (St Josemaría Escrivá)[3]

A responsible couple in love help each other grow in the virtue of chastity by practicing sexual continence, which is a proof of their love and respect for each other. They learn to be faithful and to look forward to receiving each other in a pure act of self-giving, untarnished by selfish considerations. Signs of affection specific to conjugal love are for the married state alone. Courtship upholds esteem for the beloved and, as the relationship develops, a real desire to preserve the best of one's self for the other. For this reason, in the course of getting acquainted, it is the spiritual side of the couple that must play the more active role. Only in this way can their personalities complement each other. If the relationship is clean and wholesome, then the couple will not be constrained from revealing their innermost selves, which brings about mutual knowledge and leads to deeper union, more understanding, more appreciation and more respect. They know that total

[2] Cf. Pontifical Council for the Family, *Preparation for Marriage*, 13 May 1996.
[3] *Conversations with Msgr. Escrivá*, Sinag-tala, no. 105.

union will only happen when they get married; only then will their relationship possess the full force of unconditional love.

Needless to say, a man and a woman at this stage of their relationship should deal with each other within the proper limits. People who are in love do not have to experience "everything" to get to know one another. Any premature and uncontrolled show of affection can only create undue pressure. At this stage, love should not involve complete physical surrender because otherwise it would lose its true spiritual value and cease to be genuine human love as well. Passion would have the upper hand and the marriage which the couple looks forward to would be put in jeopardy. No one should seek pleasure in sex without undertaking the commitment and responsibility of a lifelong partnership. Should a man try to possess a woman outside of the married state, without the genuine, total self giving that is possible only in marriage, the relationship would degenerate into a selfish game. Respect for the dignity of the other person would be lost and infidelity and bitterness would set in.[4] Courtship therefore has rules that must always be observed if it is to be lived in a Christian manner. The man and the woman have a serious responsibility in this regard because they owe it to themselves, to their future marriage, to the children they will later have, and most of all, to God. Love is not a game and the body is not an object of pleasure.

Getting into sexual relations outside of marriage is therefore a serious disorder because it directly violates the nature of the sexual act as a genuine gift of the spouses to one other. Stripped of the totality and exclusivity proper to the spousal union, the sexual act becomes a lie and reflects the immaturity of the couple engaging in it. In other words, what their bodies communicate does not correspond to reality; in this case, real, objective commitment does not yet exist. This is not a question of how firmly or sincerely two people commit themselves to premature intimacies. Such a relationship does not guarantee sincerity and fidelity, much less shield the two from their own shifting passions. Worse, what is most ignored are the consequences on the children born of such a relationship. Pregnancy here is avoided at all costs; and abortion becomes a common and easy way out. But even if the couple decide to have the baby, this child would be deprived of a stable environment wherein he can

[4] "...it is only by viewing sex in its natural integrity that we come to see marriage as the only adequate expression of sexual love. Respecting the integrity of sex does not mean merely concern for biological or physiological integrity. It means respect for the human wholeness of sex. Love in its sexual expression is a longing for unreserved self-giving by two people who desire to belong to each other completely in lifelong love and sharing of life, and who desire to love together into life [sic] children who will be the living image of their two-in-oneness. This is why it is only in marriage that sex finds its true personalist meaning and value and its human wholeness. Every form of sexual immorality can be defined by its deliberate exclusion of one or other aspect of this human wholeness of sexual love." *Christian Marriage*, Pastoral Letter of the Irish Episcopate, Lent 1969, no. 9.

properly grow and find the means to integrate himself into society.[5]

We cannot deny that the widespread eroticism in our times makes it more difficult, though not impossible, to ensure a clean love during courtship. The environment in most places is hostile to anything that demands effort, self-denial, and courage; anyone who strives to live a chaste life must be ready to face fierce opposition. Consider the extent to which women are being exploited and how sex is used to market anything, from eye drops to cars, with complete disregard for personal dignity. In the press, radio, film, and television, hardly any sector is exempt from such tricks, under the pretext of freedom of expression. There is a terrible confusion between love and sexual passion. These relentless attacks against sound morals have so conditioned the minds of the young that it is almost impossible for them to reflect upon the spiritual values with calm and clear judgment.

Going steady calls for serious responsibility, but many have converted this period for Christian and human development into one of vain self-affirmation and freewheeling sensuality. It is about time to rediscover the human dynamism of courtship and thus rescue it from any banal purposes. The wealth that the marriage bond and of the concomitant sacrament have to offer, as well as the clear and solid decision that a steady-dating couple make are reasons enough to seek substantial guidance. Where true love exists, pleasure

[5] See Pontifical Council for the Family, *The Truth and Meaning of Human Sexuality: Guidelines for Education within the Family*, Catholic Bishops' Conference of the Philippines, 1996, nos. 8-11.

hardly takes center stage. One can then seriously doubt the sincerity of a love professed if the constant pursuit of sensual gratification gets in the way. Such an attitude reveals selfishness coated in sweet words.

Faced with overwhelming pressure from hedonistic environments, parents and steady couples with an upright conscience usually doubt about "how far" one should go. The influence of the environment can lead to conformity and a behavior that is beneath one's dignity. As a consequence, real love can even be put to question when it is not shown through some form of physical intimacy.

"Obviously, he loves you a lot," a priest once told a young woman who was engaged to someone who respected the refinements of love during courtship. Yet she was confused. "Father, I think God has answered my prayers. I have come to doubt my boyfriend's love for me because my friends' boyfriends behave in a different way. I have been asking God to give me a clear sign that he loves me. And you come along with the answer without my asking you. Thank you."

Just like this girl who values her purity, any one who wishes to get moral issues straight ought to be forewarned that mutual feelings do not justify every-thing. The hackneyed phrase, "Show me that you love me," becomes pure fallacy when the "proof" implies physical surrender. There are many other kinds of love which are no less genuine but have nothing to do with sexual pleasure. Fraternal love, the love between friends, the love of parents for their children are just as real and as beautiful, but do not go down to the level of the sensual; they go much farther than that. They seek out the person for himself, in his inner wealth and value. Simply put, people relate to each other at different levels. The level of confidence and intimacy between husband and wife is different from that of an engaged couple, while an engaged couple can relate to each other more openly and sincerely than two people who have just met and who hardly know each other. Every situation has its limits and conditions. Thus steady dating couples do not have the right to have sex; outside of marriage, this will always be illicit. This is why Christian prudence recommends a short engagement period that will at the same time allow for a deep mutual acquaintance. Still, the realities of this new century put forth undeniably valid reasons to extend the courtship period. These include financial difficulties and the high cost of living, and one or the other partner starting off in a new career or flying off to another state or to a foreign country for graduate studies.

Frequently, teen-agers and young adults desire a quasi-matrimonial kind of commitment. They may be dead serious about it, but their age and objective conditions paint an all together different picture. They may rule out the marital act, yet they think that the firmness of their commitment would justify intimacies and exchanges that go beyond mere friendship. They are obviously wrong. Such gestures of affection would be imprudent if the said couple's situation in life is not going to change for a length of time, say, if both are students. If they habitually engage in such intimacies, they expose themselves to pressures and obligations which they are not prepared to face and which can damage their relationship and blind their conscience to the truth. And so when mom, dad, a priest or a friend dissuades them from seeing each other, this is not a sign of bad will or suspicion or malice. On the contrary, they pose a realistic and prudent warning, which is a sign of their love and concern. For this, one ought to be grateful, that is, if one really wishes dignity and respect to reign in one's relationship.

Logically, things change a bit when the persons involved have objective marks of stability, such as age, a steady job, and mature self-knowledge. They can rightly show their love for each other, as long as these gestures are clean and refined and do not directly seek sexual satisfaction; they are ready to get out of situations that can lead to engaging in the marital act. We are looking at gestures of love that show the unique respect which two unmarried persons who are in love have for each other. Compare this to a person who has been elected to public office. He may have the valid accreditation to be the president of a country, but he can only exercise his functions fully when he is legitimately sworn into the position.

Similarly, pre-marital sex contradicts the nature of sex as an act which is legitimized and authenticated by matrimony, the definitive self-giving of one person to another. In this intimate act, the body, speaking in a language all its own, confirms this total self-giving and rejects any possibility of it being short-term or temporary. Outside this context, the sexual act would be a lie and a sign of immaturity because the body is confirming something that does not exist and which has nothing to do with the lives of the ones who engage in it.

This should explain why married couples who engaged in pre-marital relations soon discover that they never got to know each other well. A relationship ruled by passion clouds the mind and maims the will: one loses the freedom to love. The sense of touch is not enough to discover a person's qualities and defects, which can bring about disconcertment, frustration and a "falling out." We have said that courtship is a period of getting personally acquainted; and this is possible only when the couple use their mind to guide their will and thus freely decide whether or not they should go on with their relationship. *That is why, each one of you know how to control his own body in holiness and honor, not in the passion of lust like heathen who do not know God.*[6]

Experience shows that separation and divorce are more frequent among those who have had sexual relations before getting married. Common sense and experience show that every pre-marital relationship causes a crack in the foundation of a future marriage; and habitual behavior in this regard constitutes a veritable time bomb for matrimonial fidelity and stability. It is not easy to give one's self wholly when one has been giving out bits and pieces of himself on a provisional basis. This partly mars the matrimonial consent as one cannot really guarantee to stay on when the results of not getting to know each other well, like pain, struggle, difficulties and misunderstanding, set in. It is therefore a good idea to hammer in the above-mentioned ideas. Far from forming a negative perception of human sexuality, chastity lived during courtship reaffirms its dignity. Instead of simply observing a list

[6] 1 Thes 4:4-5.

of taboos when it comes to showing their love for each other, the steady couple recognizes that they are preserving their dignity as persons and the natural order desired by the Creator.

The words of John Paul II throw light on the matter: "Consequently, sexuality, by means of which man and woman give themselves to one another through the acts which are proper and exclusive to spouses, is by no means something purely biological, but concerns the innermost being of the human person as such. It is realized in a truly human way only if it is an integral part of the love by which a man and a woman commit themselves totally to one another until death. The total physical self-giving would be a lie if it were not the sign and fruit of a total personal self-giving, in which the whole person, including the temporal dimension, is present: if the person were to withhold something or reserve the possibility of deciding otherwise in the future, by this very fact he or she would not be giving totally.'"

LIVING CHASTITY DURING THE PERIOD OF COURTSHIP

> *'Purity?' they ask. And they smile. They are the ones who go on to marriage with worn out bodies and disillusioned souls.*
>
> (St Josemaría Escrivá)[8]

Far from remaining passive, we must struggle against the allurements of the flesh. Not doing so would be irresponsible, immature and therefore contrary to real freedom. Those who are in love must be vigilant at all times and feel personally accountable for their actions. Notwithstanding the strong outside pressure, they must always bear in mind the precepts of Christian morals and exercise their responsibility by adhering to them. The moral norms are not obstacles to human love but guidelines of behavior that tell of one's dignity as a person and the genuineness of one's love. These precepts exalt the nobility of human love which is rooted in self-giving and untarnished by selfishness. Those who keep them are mature people who are already forging their future success and stability. Thus, when faced with a choice, a couple must weigh their options carefully and choose what would make them better persons and, later on, happily married ones. Purity is a positive trait. It is the virtue of the wise and the brave.

The means to live purity are the same as those one needs to be a virtuous person; and there is no doubt that virtue is what's at stake here. These means are: the *grace of God*, without which nothing supernatural

---

[8] St J. Escriva, *The Way*, Sinag-tala, no. 120.

can be accomplished, and *constant personal effort*. But one's efforts must be properly directed. In the first place, one must *flee the occasions of sin*, and this takes a great amount of sincerity because it is easy to fool one's self. Certain environments easily pose temptations to sin. These include solitary areas where a couple can be alone in a car, movie houses that shamelessly exhibit pornographic films, and night spots where people take hard drinks or drugs. Add to these a fool-hardy sense of confidence and those unchecked caresses. Small wonder people find it hard to live their court-ship in a truly Christian way. Parents have the duty to forewarn their adolescent children about the dangers imprudence brings. They must educate their children in purity to avoid regrettable mistakes in the future.

One likewise needs a *strong will*. Impressive argu-ments are useless when a person is accustomed to yielding to the smallest insinuations of pleasure, or who moves in an environment where he can easily give in to every whim. He has become a slave of his passions. One's will needs to be strengthened because through it, the human person can choose the good and thus be truly free and able to follow the dictates of an upright conscience. To educate the will, one must learn to live a spirit of self-denial, keep one's sight in check, and fight against softness of character. Likewise, one must strive for self-mastery and not allow himself to be swayed by external circumstances. One ought to be in control of the circumstances around him and direct his life toward concrete goals that will perfect him humanly as well as supernaturally.[9]

[9] "Take very special care of chastity and also of the other

It is also important to *form one's conscience*. Passion often blurs judgment and one can easily deceive himself without a clear set of ideas and a proper scale of values to refer to. Man's reason steers him to a specific goal, and prevents him from being sidetracked by some momentary impulse.[10] Lastly, we must bear in mind that no human being is perfect. We are all prone to error and everyone has his own share of mistakes. We do fail in many things and, when this happens, we must acknowledge our shortcomings and humbly bear the consequences of our fallen nature. Mistakes, however, must be corrected since to regard them as irreparable would be to despair. It is always possible

virtues which accompany it: modesty and refinement. They are as it were the safeguard of chastity. Don't take lightly those norms of conduct which help so much to keep us worthy in the sight of God: keeping a watchful guard over our senses and our heart; the courage—the courage to be a coward—to flee from the occasions of sin; going to the sacraments frequently, particularly to the sacrament of Confession; complete sincerity in our own spiritual direction; sorrow, contrition, and reparation after one's falls. And all this imbued with a tender devotion to Our Lady so that she may obtain for us from God the gift of a clean and holy life." St Josemaría Escrivá, *Friends of God*, Sinag-tala Publishers, no. 185.

[10] "We must be as clean and pure as we can as far as the body is concerned and without being afraid, because sex is something noble and holy—a participation in God's creative power—which was made for marriage. And thus, pure and fearless, you will give testimony by your behavior that it is possible and beautiful to live holy purity. First, we will strive to refine our conscience. We must go sufficiently deep, until we can be sure our conscience is well formed and we can distinguish between a delicate conscience, which is a true grace from God, and a scrupulous conscience, which is not the same." *Ibid.*

to begin anew. What is important is to recognize what the human body is. *Do you not know that your body is a temple of the Holy Spirit within you, which you have from God? You are not your own; you were brought with a price. So glorify God in your body.*[11]

It is impossible to live a clean life without the help of God. Christians can always rely on the grace of the sacraments, especially that of Penance and the Holy Eucharist. The former is a sign of the love of God who is ever ready to forgive and to welcome the repentant sinner, no matter how great his sin may be. In the Eucharist, the very Author of grace offers himself as nourishment and guarantees to help us in our struggle to live our faith. Through grace and constant personal effort couples are assured of living an ideal courtship period, the best preparation for a happy and blessed married life.

THINGS TO TAKE INTO ACCOUNT

Many factors must be considered before jumping into a commitment as big as marriage. For instance, educators generally discourage steady dating at an *early age* because adolescents need a social life to develop their personality; and a premature romantic commitment often cuts one's contact with boys and girls of one's age. A boy's masculinity and a girl's femininity develop through friendship, and even conflicts, with persons of the same sex. Hence, one generally loses much by going steady too soon. Another

[11] 1 Cor 6:19-20.

disadvantage is the risk of a long courtship period wherein the adolescent couple expose themselves to unnecessary pressure and obligations during this critical period of their life; again, this has an impact on the development of their personality. Finally, the young couple have to reckon with stronger temptations because they are still grappling with their own passions and sense of identity; thus the risk of an early marriage. In this event, the chances of a break-up are greater because they are not mature enough to take on the challenges of married life.

A man and a woman must also be compatible insofar as *life principles* are concerned. Religion, social and ethnic background, and outlook in life certainly have a great deal to do with the outcome of a marriage. Similarly, differences in family and social upbringing, especially if the gap is significant, can be a source of discord. This however does not justify that parents be unreasonably opposed to their children marrying someone of a different race or social background. We must always bear in mind that all men are equal before God. The color of one's skin, one's economic condition or one's educational background, by itself, does not justify parental opposition to their children's choice of a marriage partner.

There are many other areas to look into. For example, the little disagreements that are willingly overlooked during courtship but which become a source of constant quarrels after the couple gets married. Some-times, it may not occur to either one to talk about it. Not that they are insincere, but simply because the matter seems too trivial. Nevertheless, with the passing of time what is trivial now can be blown up later and even seriously threaten the peace in the home. For this, steady couples are well advised to carefully consider the small things that bother them or cause them to have second thoughts about each other. In this way, they avert the danger of discovering that, with the passing of years and the constant contact brought about by married life, they cannot live together in harmony. Sometimes, people in love are so naïve to think that small differences will disappear after they get married. They do not realize that what seems small now tends to look much bigger later; and today's slight annoyances usually become unbearable tomorrow. The couple must therefore face up to the causes of their quarrels now and then decide to change or to accept each other's defects, along with the lifelong consequences of their decision. Otherwise, it would be better to break up and look for someone else now rather than risk an unhappy union that will last a lifetime.

We have laid down general applications, and the engaged couple may not wholly identify with them. Nevertheless, we invite those who are thinking of getting married to review them carefully. Freedom in this case calls for a clear mind and the capacity and willingness to take on a responsibility of great magnitude. Prudence dictates that a person seeks advice. And even if one's parents have no right to interfere in a personal decision, they are usually objective when it comes to analyzing a situation. For one thing, parents count on longer experience; and God has given them a special grace to guide their children wisely.

THE PARENTS' ROLE

Prudence plays an important role in decision-making. And prudence demands that one listens to advice. Parents have to respect their children's decision even if they disagree with it, but this does not stop them from properly guiding their children's desires and ambitions, perhaps even seriously pointing out facts that may weigh against the decision already made. Parents should be in the best position to calmly and positively explain to their children the basics of Christian marriage—its vocational character and indissolubility, and the illicitness of premarital sex, abortion, and artificial contraception. They can be a great help in discerning the conditions needed to establish a serious and honest marriage bond and in helping their child give a clear testimony of Christian life to his or her future spouse.[12]

Nevertheless, we insist that parents should not impose themselves, directly or indirectly, on their children's choice of partner. They can only point out certain disadvantages that their child probably does not see. And they must never get angry or withdraw themselves from a child who refuses to take their advice. Psychological warfare of this kind will not stop the wedding; instead, it brings unnecessary suffering to a fledgling home that needs all the support possible to get ahead. Those "I do's" have to be exchanged in an atmosphere of peace and serenity; only in this way can the newlyweds feel fully responsible for their actions.

[12] Cf. Augusto Sarmiento, *La integración de la sexualidad en el bien de la persona*, *Scripta Teológica* 31 (1999/3), pp. 677-713.

MORE USEFUL POINTS TO PONDER[13]

It is very advisable for a pre-teener to know the deep significance of marriage, understood as a union of love whose goal is the total, personal development of the spouses and the procreation and education of the children. *Self-mastery, formation of character and a spirit of sacrifice* are therefore indispensable to achieving stable conjugal love; more so amidst the prevailing confusion in present-day society.

Preparation for family life is an important aspect of human education because the family is the primordial base where one learns to love, and for the right ends and reasons. The value of human sexuality lies in its links with other human values. As a vital force, it unites man and woman to form a *family*. The *fruitfulness* of the sexual act underscores the fecundity of the human body and the mystery of *procreation* wherein new life is born from the intimacy of the married couple. Human sexuality celebrates the marvel and mystery of life—one's own and that of others—from the moment of conception. It also highlights the *transcendent union* of man, as husband and father, and woman, as wife and mother, which is above all spiritual and without which sex loses its human meaning. Finally, it upholds the family as the necessary foundation for the growth and development of all its members. All these are the wealth of human sexuality.[14]

[13] Cf. Pontifical Commission for the Family, *Preparing for Marriage*, 13 May 1996. See also Javier Abad-Gomez, *El noviazgo y su relación con la dignidad de la persona* in *Viviendo el amor*, Aspaen, Bogotá, 1997.

[14] Cf. Víctor García Hoz, *Pedagogía visible y educación invisible*, Ediciones Rialp, Madrid, 1987, 50.

It is also good to know correct and complete information about a married couple's responsibilities as regards the number of children they should have. More than anything else, responsible parenthood is knowing how to discern the morality of the various methods of birth control with the aim of being open to the fullness of love and life. John Paul II insists that the natural methods of regulating births should be clearly explained and disseminated. "Accordingly, every effort must be made to render such knowledge accessible to all married people and also to young adults before marriage through clear, timely and serious instruction and education given by married couples, doctors and experts."[15] Nowadays, the scientific soundness of the natural methods of regulating fertility has been fully proven and it is very useful to know what these are. A couple may resort to these methods for just reasons, however these must never be reduced to mere technique but rather be seen as a way to educate the couple in virtue and therefore to love each other more. Thus it is the virtue of chastity that moves the couple to practice periodic sexual continence.[16]

Wedding preparations ought to include the engaged couple's education in the natural demands that married persons should meet within the context of God's plan. These are: an awareness that freedom of consent is the foundation of the marital bond; that this bond is one and indissoluble; that responsible parenthood means being open to the children God wants them to have; that sex within marriage has its human aspects; and

[15] FC 33.
[16] Cf. *Catechism of the Catholic Church* ECCCE Word & Life Publications, Manila 1994, 2366-2371

that the sexual act has its demands and goals, which are the procreation and education of children. All these requires formation of conscience and knowledge of basic psychological, pedagogical and medico-legal concepts related to marriage and the family. But what matters most is that the couple deepen their knowledge of the moral and theological underpinnings of self-giving and responsible parenthood because conjugal love is one that is total, exclusive, faithful, and fruitful.

Such preparation will also guarantee that the engaged couple have clear ideas about matrimony, the roles proper to a married couple as a family and in society, and about human sexuality and openness to others. It is likewise obvious that each spouse will have certain shortcomings—psychological or affective—that may hinder one from relating with others, as well as selfish attitudes that can water down one's total commitment to the other. Knowing these shortcomings will also bring about a discovery of each other's strengths and therefore both spouses will end up encouraging each other to be better persons. But for this, they must have an informed moral conscience so that they may enter into the conjugal pact with a free and decisive spirit.

The end product of this period of preparation will be a clear awareness of the essential points of the marital commitment. These are:

unity;
fidelity;
indissolubility;
fecundity;
a coherent life;

life in the spirit, thanks to the grace which makes the Christian spouses both the subjects and ministers of this sacrament that symbolizes Christ's love for the Church;

and availability to carry out the mission proper to families in society and as members of the Church.

The proximate preparation should include a deepening of the life of faith and a rediscovery of the sacraments and the life of prayer. "The religious formation of the young couple should be integrated at the right moment and in accordance with the various concrete requirements, with a preparation for life as a couple. This preparation will present marriage as an interpersonal relationship of a man and a woman that has to be continually developed and it will encourage those concerned to study the nature of conjugal sexuality and responsible parenthood with the essential medical and biological knowledge connected with it. It will also acquaint those concerned with correct methods for the education of children, and will assist them in gaining the basic requisite for well-ordered family life, sensible administration, notions of housekeeping. Finally, one must not overlook preparation for the family apostolate, for fraternal solidarity and collaboration with other families, for active membership in groups, associations, movements and undertakings set up for the human and Christian benefit of the family." [17]

[17] FC 66.

Of transcendental importance is that the future spouses learn to nurture their love in the face of the ups and downs of living together, and know how to overcome inevitable crises through open and sincere dialogue. At the heart of a Christian couple's preparation for marriage is a reflection on the Faith through the Word of God and the guidance of the Magisterium of the Church regarding the sacrament. They must be aware that they are "one flesh"[18] in Christ by the power of the Holy Spirit. This means that their existence is imprinted with a new character apart from that which they received in Baptism. The sacrament of Matrimony transforms their love into a concrete expression of Christ's love for his Church. And in the light of the sacrament, each act of the spouses—that is, the procreative act, their action as educators of their children, the daily experience of living together, their apostolate, and their involvement in society—is a privileged moment in their life as Christians. For even if they have not yet received the sacrament, Christ already sustains and accompanies the engaged couple in their course of living a life of grace and in their growing participation in the mystery of the Church.

This is why it is good for today's engaged couples to educate themselves and to fine-tune their sense of values when it comes to defending life. The contraceptive mentality predominates in many places, despising human life from womb to tomb. Such is the attack against the family that it cannot carry out its most

---

[18] Mt 19:6.

intimate mission, much less develop in accordance with what constitutes authentic human growth.[19] We look to the day that they will be able to contribute to the building of a culture of life through their innate respect for and welcoming of love in the form of a new human life. Thus the married couple testifies to, celebrates and serves humanity.[20] Marriage is an adventure of love that is well worth pursuing as a way to earthly happiness and as a foretaste of heaven promised to those who have struggled to be faithful, and won—to the very gates of death.

[19] John Paul II, Enc. *Centesimus annus* 39.
[20] John Paul II, Enc. *Evangelium vitae* 83-84, 86, 93.

2

Marriage as a Vocation

God's Plans for Marriage

To explain the *originality* of matrimony as a natural institution, John Paul II[1] explains that when God created man in his image and likeness, he called him into existence out of love and at the same time calls him to love. Sacred Scripture[2] says that God is love and lives a mysterious interior communion of love. Now, since man and woman are created in the divine image, their very nature bears the vocation to love: the capacity and the responsibility to give themselves and to engage in an interpersonal communion. Love then is a vocation that is basic and intrinsic to all human beings.

As an incarnate spirit, man is called to love in the totality of his being; thus the human body participates in and is embraced by this spiritual love. And this is why the sexual act, whereby a man and a woman give

[1] *FC* 11, 18-19.
[2] 1 Jn 4:8.

themselves to each other in a manner proper and exclusive to spouses, is not a purely biological phenomenon; it affects the intimate core of the person as such. The act then is truly human only when it becomes an integral part of the love between a man and a woman who totally committed to each other till death; otherwise, the physical gift would be a deception. If a person holds back on something, like the possibility of changing one's mind in the future, then the sexual act would not be a sign and fruit of total self-giving—which includes one's bodily dimension.

Consequently, matrimony is the only place where such total self-giving can happen. Here, a man and a woman establish a contract based on their free and conscious decision to form an intimate community of life and love which God himself desired. Only in this light does the sexual act become truly meaningful. The institution of marriage is not an undue social or bureaucratic imposition, but a true vocation. Here, a private pact is confirmed in public as unique and exclusive so that it may be realized in completely fidelity to the plans of the Divine Creator. And far from diminishing human freedom, fidelity shields the pact against any form of subjective or relativist reasoning and makes it participate in the wisdom of the Creator.

God is the origin of Matrimony. It is not a product of chance or of the evolution of blind forces. It is a natural institution that is profoundly rooted in man's very nature and whose aim is that the spouses carry out a project of love, desired by the Creator himself, through their reciprocal and exclusive self giving. Jesus Christ himself explains to his disciples the divine origins of marriage so that they may understand that if a man and a woman freely unite themselves in marriage, then there can be no substitute for their free consent. Still man ought to respect the innate nature, constitutive norms, and inherent ends and obligations of marriage. In a word, man must respect the particular mission entrusted to the spouses. *Have you not read that he who made them from the beginning made them male and female, and said, 'For this reason a man shall leave his father and mother and be joined to his wife, and the two shall become one?' So they are no longer two but one.*[3] Marriage is not a human, but a divine invention. Nevertheless, people can perfectly choose whether they should get married or not, each one to his own call. And if it is to begin a shared life of love and fruitfulness, then one must realize that he is answering a call to carry out a specific supernatural trust.

"The Creator himself desires this communion of life that you have freely and responsibly accepted. It is a communion of life whose norms God has not left to the free judgment of men; it must be lived, rather, in conformity with the divine plan. And for the welfare of mankind, God himself has made marriage an indissoluble bond between one man and one woman. Fill up your hearts then with confidence and serenity. In the measure your marriage is lived in filial union with the Lord and in prayer, you will never lack the means to carry out your lofty mission. And, even here on earth, you will experience those true joys of the heart that no one will be able to take away from you."[4]

[3] Mt 19:3.
[4] John Paul II, *Address to Newlyweds*, Rome, 7 February 1979.

Moreover, God made man a social being—that is, he needs to communicate and to be with others. *Then the Lord God said, 'It is not good that the man should be alone; I will make him a helper fit for him.'*[5] And man and woman were called to fulfill a concrete divine duty which is to carry on the creative act through the generation of new human beings, in solidarity with God himself. *So God created man in his own image, in the image of God he created him; male and female he created them. And God blessed them, and God said to them, 'Be fruitful and multiply, and fill the earth and subdue it.'*[6]

The family, founded on and strengthened by love is a community of persons: the husband, the wife, their children and all their relatives. Its first task is to make the communion of love a reality through the constant effort to develop an authentic community of persons. The interior principle or permanent force and the ultimate goal of the family's task is love. Thus, without love the family is not a community of persons; and without love the family cannot live, develop and perfect itself as a community of persons. The love of the spouses and, in an extended way, the love of parents and children, brothers and sisters, and relatives, is driven by an inner dynamism that leads to a more profound and intense communion which is the soul and foundation of the community of marriage and the family.

The spouses initiate and develop this communion of love. By virtue of their pact of love, a man and a woman *are no longer two but one*[7] and are called to

___

[5] Gen 2:18.
[6] Gen 1:27-28.
[7] Mt 19:6; Gen 2:24.

continually grow in communion by being faithful each day to their vows to live a total, reciprocal donation. The conjugal communion is rooted in the fact that man and woman naturally complement each other, and it is nourished by the spouses' willingness to share a lifetime of what they are and what they have. This is why such a communion is the fruit and the sign of a deeply profound human need. In addition, Christ our Lord gathers to himself this need and confirms, purifies and elevates it to the perfection of a sacrament. He infuses the Holy Spirit into its celebration and offers the Christian spouses a gift of new communion of love which is the living and true image of the singular union that exists in the Church, the undivided Mystical Body of the Lord Jesus.

This is why, for Christian spouses, this gift of the Holy Spirit is a commandment of life and an impulse for them to aim at a deeper union in body, character, heart and soul, mind and will. In this way they manifest to the Church and to the world the new communion of love which they received by the grace of Christ. As such, this communion is radically opposed to polygamy. Polygamy violates God's plans which he had revealed from the start: that man and woman have an equal personal dignity and that they give themselves to each other in matrimony with one, total and exclusive love. "Firmly established by the Lord, the unity of marriage will radiate from the equal personal dignity of wife and husband, a dignity acknowledged by mutual and total love."[8]

---

[8] *Gaudium et spes* 49; See also John Paul II, *Discourse to Spouses*, Kinshasa, 3 May 1980, no. 4.

Marriage is a True Vocation

"For a Christian, marriage is not just a social institution, much less a mere remedy for human weakness. It is a real supernatural calling. A great sacrament, in Christ and in the Church, says St Paul. At the same time, it is a permanent contract between a man and a woman. Whether we like it or not, the sacrament of matrimony, instituted by Christ, cannot be dissolved. It is a permanent contract that sanctifies in cooperation with Jesus Christ. He fills the souls of husband and wife and invites them to follow him. He transforms their whole married life into an occasion for God's presence on earth."[9]

Many think that marriage is meant only to satisfy the needs of our nature—the need for physical satisfaction and the need to love and be loved. Hardly does it occur to people that marriage can be closely linked with God's plans for a person. At best it could be a way for spouses to render God some service and an opportunity to do his Will by fulfiling the duties of the married state. But a vocation? Never would the thought have crossed their minds. And yet marriage is a vocation. It is a divine summons which demands a positive response from those who are called to this state. It entails a God-given mission which married couples are expected to fulfil throughout their entire lives.

People at times speak of marriage as something of a lesser evil when it comes to seeking sanctity—something perhaps of a leftover for those who have not been fortunate enough to receive any vocation to serve

[9] *Christ is Passing By* no. 23.

God. Nothing could be farther from the truth: apostolic celibacy, the religious professions, the married life, and the priestly ministry are all vocations from God. Each man is led to discover his vocation in the time and manner fore-ordained by Providence; and what matters most is that, once this vocation has been discovered, a person follows it with an upright intention and devotes his whole heart to its fulfillment. Only in this way will his energies and talents be properly spent at the service of God and neighbor.

God has a plan for each one. He intervenes in a direct and immediate manner in the creation of every soul and gives to each person a specific mission to accomplish, a concrete task to fulfill. This is what the vocation is. It is the loving design of God conceived for every human being from all eternity.

Some—relatively few in number—are chosen by God to receive very special graces and to collaborate with him in a more direct way in the work of Redemption. God asks them to surrender themselves to him completely and to be absolutely detached from all earthly loves. From among them, some are called to abandon the world and enter the religious life; others are destined to become priests and to identify themselves in a sacramental way with Christ, the Head of the Church. Others still are meant to live a life of apostolic celibacy in the midst of the world, sanctifying temporal realities and rendering a supernatural service to their fellow men. From all of them God expects fidelity. He wants them to persevere in their commitment of self-surrender and to channel their best energies to its lifelong fulfillment. God will give them the grace they need to be faithful and, with their correspondence to this grace, they will surely accomplish their divine mission.

There are many other kinds of vocations apart from those described above; and marriage is one of them. Since getting married already comes so naturally to a person, one usually does not expect special signs from heaven to confirm a calling to this state. This does not mean, however, that matrimony has a secondary role in the work of Redemption, that it is merely a natural phenomenon and involves no divine calling of its own. Matrimony—it must be affirmed—is a genuine divine vocation. It involves a mission that God entrusts to man. For Christians, it is a sacrament—a supernatural reality that brings with it special graces that enable the spouses to carry out their duties faithfully. Through marriage, Christian husbands and wives take part in God's plans to redeem all men and it is in this state that they should strive to become saints.

Every vocation is a calling to accomplish some specific mission. It demands a concrete response, a willingness to be God's instrument to carry out freely and responsibly the task one has been entrusted with. As a consequence, it alone gives divine meaning to our existence, a meaning we will never lose so long as we accept our vocation with generosity and live up to its demands with fidelity.

Couples often do not realize that their "I do's" are in fact an answer to a divine call. Very frequently, their idea of marriage is something taken straight out of the movies—it is either a sentimental affair or a carnal relationship. The first misconception is more common among women. They marry in the hope to find the sweetness of loving and the joys of being loved; they want to feel the warmth of companionship and the security of a home. Oftentimes, too, their notion of motherhood is colored by the same idea. They think of how wonderful it will be to be called "Mommy." They imagine how their children will look, and how loving and mischievous they will be. Men, on the other hand, tend toward the second error. They believe that the conjugal union is primarily an outlet for one's concupiscence or a means to satisfy one's craving for pleasure. These false impressions have led to many—a broken home. They paint an incomplete picture of married life and therefore mislead couples into expecting from marriage what marriage alone was never meant to give. A true picture of marriage must include its supernatural dimension; it must make couples understand the divine mission it brings and the lifelong effort they will have to exert to carry it out. Only such a view of marriage will enable them to appreciate its genuine meaning as a Christian vocation.

Pope John Paul II adds: "We are sometimes content, perhaps a little superficially, to consult polls or statistics—carried out, maybe, on the basis of predetermined ideologies—which collect aspects that are changeable and can also be manipulated, the reflection, in turn, of changing situations of a cultural, sociological, political, and economic character...Let us not forget that behind so many analyses and statistical data, there is a great vacuum which surround persons who, as a matter of fact, are confessing their own solitude, their own moral and spiritual emptiness, because they have not been sufficiently educated in the true meaning of the matrimonial union and of family life as a vocation to a fruitful, unique and unrepeatable experience of communication in harmony with God's initial and permanent plan—a vocation from which there spring, of course, serious duties and responsibilities to which it is necessary to be faithful, for the sake of the children and in obedience to divine commands."[10]

A Call to Total Self-surrender

Couples who come to understand marriage as a divine vocation naturally find in this discovery the great stimulus to generously undertake the mission entrusted to them. They see more clearly the need to fulfill to the best of their ability all their duties as married persons. They realize, too, that their best efforts must be directed, above all, to giving themselves completely to their spouse—a goal that demands self-denial, self-forgetfulness, and a willingness to forego personal likes and preferences for the sake of the other. "Love has certain standard features. Sometimes we speak of love as if it were an impulse to self-satisfaction or a mere means to selfish fulfillment of one's own personality. But that's not love. True love means going out of oneself, giving oneself. Love brings joy, but a joy whose roots are in the shape of a cross. As long as we are on earth and have not yet arrived at the fullness of the future life, we can never have true love without sacrifice and pain.[11]

---

[10] *Address to the Bishops of Venezuela*, 15 November 1979.
[11] St J. Escrivá, *op. cit.*, no. 43.

Marriage, therefore, means a lifelong commitment of genuine self-surrender. It calls for humility, fortitude, a spirit of sacrifice, and docility to the graces which God always grants when they are asked for with simplicity. Husband and wife will be happy together if they learn to overcome selfishness and love of comfort, if they avoid seeking personal compensations for every sacrifice they make, and if they know how to give without expecting anything in return. To achieve all this, it will greatly help them to remember that whatever they do for the love of their spouse is reckoned by Christ as actually done to himself. *And the King will answer them, Truly, I say to you, as you did it to one of the least of these my brethren, you did it to me.*[12]

From the very start, couples must be aware that sacrifice borne willingly is the key to a happy marriage. It is with cheerful hearts that spouses give themselves to each other, deeply convinced that life on earth—as Scripture would have it—*is a warfare*.[13] They must remember that sacrifice is what ennobles a person. It is what makes one mature and rise to the heights of virtue—for only man can set noble goals for himself, climb the narrow road to true happiness, and share at the same time his joy and good companionship with others. Of all creatures, only man can grasp that "beyond strict duty is the divine invitation to generosity."[14] "The constant fulfillment of the duties of this Christian vocation demands notable virtue. For this reason, strengthened by grace for holiness of life, the couple

[12] Mt 25: 40.
[13] Cf. Job 7:1.
[14] Elvira Jaramillo de Botero, unpublished work, Manizales, 1999.

will painstakingly cultivate and pray for steadiness in love, large-heartedness and the spirit of sacrifice."[15]

The Magisterium of the Church teaches that the purpose of marriage lies in the begetting and upbringing of children, the personal enrichment of the spouses, and the help they render each other. As a vocation that demands love, it necessarily leads one to "complicate" one's life, as some would put it, for the sake of God. This is the way, however, that leads the spouses to truly love each other and to identify themselves with Christ's new commandment: *Love one another as I have loved you.*[16] This is how the love of the spouses opens the door to God's love; and children are the fruit of this love. Children are God's gift to parents who freely and intelligently cooperate with him to bring new life into the world. This is how God wishes to and develop and increase the number of his children on earth— men and women who will act as divine leaven for the Christian transformation of society. Truly then, the fecund love between the spouses reflects the intimate union between Christ and his Church, and the spiritual and apostolic fruits that this union brings.

[15] *GS* 49.
[16] Jn 15:12.

3

The Love Between Spouses

"The family, which is founded and given life by love, is a community of persons: of husband and wife, of parents and children, of relatives. Its first task is to live with fidelity the reality of communion in a constant effort to develop an authentic community of persons.

The inner principle of the task, its permanent power and its final goal is love: without love the family is not a community of persons and, in the same way, *without love the family cannot live, grow and perfect itself as a community of persons.*"

(John Paul II)[1]

Love, no doubt, is the most beautiful experience a person can have. It makes one happy and fulfilled, it expands the heart and ennobles one's entire life. Man is capable of doing great things for love, the way good parents or spouses or friends make sacrifices for the people they most love. They do not think they are doing anything special but take delight in generously

---

[1] *FC* 18.

giving themselves. By loving and being "in love," all of a person's potentials, one's entire existence, are fulfilled to the utmost. As the Pope beautifully puts it, "Man cannot live without love. He remains a being that is incomprehensible for himself, his life is senseless if love is not revealed to him, if he does not encounter love, if he does not experience it and make it his own, if he does not participate intimately in it."[2] And Sacred Scripture has sung of it from antiquity: *Set me a seal upon your heart as a seal upon your arm; for love is strong as death, jealousy is cruel as the grave. Its flashes are flashes of fire, a most vehement flame. Many waters cannot quench love, neither can floods drown it. If a man offered for love all the wealth of his house, it would be utterly scorned.*[3]

As a *seal* emblazoned on the arm, love moves one to make his own the heart of the other and to place all his strength at the service of the beloved. This love is *as strong as death*, oblivious of obstacles and relentlessly pursuing its object. Its *flashes of fire* give light and warmth to the life of the lovers, a fire which neither the flood of problems that swamp daily life nor the unforeseen winds of contradiction can extinguish. Thus, *if a man offered for love all the wealth of his house, it would be utterly scorned*: all the energy, effort and sacrifice spent to obtain this great good seem little or nothing. This explains why marriage is called a total union of love. When a man and a woman marry, they establish an unbreakable bond of total and mutual self-giving, a love that is in no way some transient emotion or temporary passion, but a free and responsible

[2] *Redemptor hominis* 10.
[3] *Song* 8:6-7.

decision to be one—in good times and in bad. It is one's gift of self to the other.[4]

Nowadays, it is easy to confuse "feelings" for love. This is a false concept that has brought about many failed marriages. Love is not a feeling but an act of the will. To say "I love you" means "I decide to share my life with you and to give myself to you completely." Of course, feelings also come into play here, with an intensity (or the lack of it) that depends on one's temperament or on the circumstances that one is presently undergoing. In other words, one can really love without "feeling" and one can "feel" without truly loving. The elements of true love are faithfulness, understanding, generosity and sacrifice. And everybody knows that one does not love some*thing* but some*one*. Thus to love truly is to look at the entire person and at the entirety of the person: body and soul, virtues and defects, points of convergence and points of discord.

THE INTEGRAL ELEMENTS OF CONJUGAL LOVE[5]

In another address to newly married couples, the present Pope encourages husbands and wives to act in a way that their deepest joy should spring from a love that is faithful, patient, understanding, self-sacrificing and pure. Love cannot be total without fidelity, mutual harmony, generosity and patience. These are the conditions that make life together truly a wonderful experience.[6]

[4] Cf. John Paul II, *Address to Newlyweds*, 9 May 1979.
[5] Karol Wojtyla, *Love and Responsibility*, 76 ff.
[6] Cf. *Address to Newlyweds*, 12 September 1979.

The first element of conjugal love is *love as attraction*, which is that of taking pleasure in the presence of a good, that is, the discovery of the physical or spiritual attributes of a person. This pleasure comes, in the first place, from sense experience but has other elements as well: the feelings and the will. Feelings arise spontaneously, a reaction that, in the end, blinds the beholder to reality. Sometimes, the attractiveness of a person leads the beholder to perceive only an apparent good in the other: qualities that one does not really have. Hence, the moment the love of attraction fades, the initial reaction would be disillusionment, and then aversion, rejection or even hatred. Now, since the human person by nature is defined by what is "inside," one must learn to discover and to take pleasure, above all, in the inner beauty of the other.

A second element is *love as desire*, or concupiscence, which is not a negative concept, but part of the essence of love that develops between a man and a woman. Man as such is a limited being who is not satisfied being alone; he needs to be with others. In the case of conjugal love, the aspect of sexuality is a treasure, the means to give one's self to another and to be open to life. On the other hand, sexuality also expresses a limitation, which is why man and woman need each other. They are meant to complement one another. This real need is manifested in the *attraction* between sexes, which is a phenomenon that leads to love. Thus, love of desire springs from the said need and moves the person to seek a good which he or she lacks. However, this love is not limited to desires as this could simply turn the other into a mere object for one's own satisfaction. Saying "I love you as a good for myself" is different from "I desire you or your body for my own pleasure." And so one must avoid the error of reducing love as desire to mere sensual desire.

Love that does not transcend the level of desire would remain imperfect because the love of concupiscence does not exhaust the essence of love between two people. It is not enough to desire a person as a good for one's self: one must love the good for its own sake. One then advances from the stage of "I desire you as a good" to that of "I desire your good." This altruistic orientation of the heart is called *love of goodwill* or benevolent love, the third element that brings out the noblest qualities of human love and brings it close to what constitutes the pure essence of love. To achieve this, one must habitually try to acquire an attitude of benevolence. This is especially important in married life. If husband and wife strive to be generous with one another, then benevolent love can go hand-in-hand with the love of desire, even physical desire, as long as the latter does not dominate all of the wealth that human love has to offer.

A fourth element would be *reciprocal love* because love by nature is a give-and-take relationship. It is bilateral, not unilateral; it is social and interpersonal. It reaches its fullness when a man and a woman on opposite sides of the road cross over to meet and to begin talking, not about what is "mine," but about what is "ours."

THE DIFFERENT ASPECTS OF CONJUGAL LOVE

In the encyclical *Humanae vitae*, Pope Paul VI stresses the importance of knowing exactly the characteristic marks and demands of conjugal love.

"This love is first of all fully **human**, that is to say, of the senses and of the spirit at the same time. It is not, then, a simple transport of instinct and sentiment, but also and principally, an act of the free will, intended to endure and to grow by means of the joys and sorrows of daily life, in such a way that husband and wife become only one heart and only one soul, and together attain their human perfection.

Then, this love is **total**, that is to say, it is a very special form of personal friendship in which husband and wife generously share everything without undue reservations or selfish calculations. Whoever truly loves his marriage partner loves not only for what he receives, but for the partner's self, rejoicing that he can enrich his partner with the gift of himself.

Again, this love is **faithful** and **exclusive** until death. Thus, in fact, do bride and groom conceive it to be on the day when they freely and in full awareness assume the duty of the marriage bond. A fidelity which can sometimes be difficult, but is always possible, always noble and meritorious, as no one can deny. The example of so many married persons down through the centuries shows not only that fidelity is according to the nature of marriage, but also that it is a source of profound and lasting happiness.

And finally, this love is **fecund**, for it is not exhausted by the communion between husband and wife, but is destined to continue, raising up new lives."[7]

[7] *Humanae vitae* 9.

The Pope here outlines the wealth contained in conjugal love: *something that is fully human, sensible and at the same time spiritual.* It is not simply an outpouring of the instinct—which is the physical or carnal dimension—and of the sentiments—which is the affective dimension. It is also and principally an act of the will, a "wanting to"—which is the spiritual or rational dimension—, a form of personal friendship.

We can add a fourth aspect, the supernatural one, which, for Christians, is the consequence of the sacramental dimension of Matrimony. In this regard, John Paul II says: "The Spirit which the Lord pours forth gives a new heart, and renders man and woman capable of loving one another as Christ has loved us. Conjugal love reaches that fullness to which it is interiorly ordained, conjugal charity, which is the proper and specific way in which the spouses participate in and are called to live the very charity of Christ who gave himself on the Cross."[8]

Conjugal love therefore embraces the whole person, that is, in one's bodily, affective, spiritual, and supernatural dimensions. Logically, it also includes the tendency to seek a mutual relationship wherein one can give one's self to another person, to one's children, and to the love of God. Of all the human passions, love is the first, the most meaningful, and that which gives meaning to life because it embraces the human being as a whole, from one's highest spiritual aspirations to the most carnal demands of the human body. In the love of husband and wife, spirit and matter come together as equal; thus human love is the love of the entire man.

[8] *FC* 13.

Physical Love

Sexual activity is part of the divine plan to beget human life. It includes all the physical processes, expressions and reactions--instinctive in nature, arising from the mutual physical attraction between the sexes--that lead to sexual union and which produce keen sensual pleasure.

Marriage alone is the adequate situation for sexual intimacy because only in it does sex find its real personalist meaning and fulfill its role in the complete integration of two human beings. Sexual union is the climax of the affective love between spouses. It is not only a licit but a noble reality, pleasing to God and necessary to achieve perfect union between husband and wife. As such, it must express a complete giving of self, purified of egoism and all selfish calculation.

"Marriage is a sacrament that makes one flesh of two bodies. Theology expresses this fact in a striking way when it teaches us that the matter of the sacrament consists of the bodies of husband and wife. Our Lord sanctifies and blesses the mutual love of husband and wife. He foresees not only a union of souls, but also a union of bodies. No Christian, whether or not he is called to the married state, has a right to underestimate the value of marriage. We have been created by God and endowed with an intelligence which is like a spark of the divine intellect. Together with our free will, another gift of God, it allows us to know and to love God. God has also placed in our body the power to generate, which is a participation in his own creative power. He wanted to use love to bring new human beings into the world and to increase the body of the Church. Thus, sex is not a shameful thing; it is a divine gift, ordained to life, to love, to fruitfulness."[9]

The sacrament of Matrimony sanctifies and converts the physical union of the spouses into a channel of divine grace. A great mystery, indeed, and one which is clearly reflected in Sacred Scripture, where marriage figures as an image of the union between Christ and his Church—a union so intimate that the Church is sometimes referred to as Christ's Spouse and other times as his Body. Both expressions are closely linked. The Church was founded by Christ when he took on human flesh and edified it throughout his life on earth. The Risen Lord configured the community of faithful disciples after his death and glorified it when he sent the Holy Spirit on the day of Pentecost.

In this light, sexual intercourse performed in its proper context, respecting the moral order, becomes an effective channel of grace for the spouses. Nothing about it is offensive to God. He is pleased with the mutual self-giving of husband and wife and even elevates it to the supernatural order. The spouses' faith in Christ then becomes a guiding force when they give their bodies to each other. Their faith makes them see the sexual act not only as an eminently positive reality that enhances their personalities, but also as a channel of grace which sanctifies their union. Thus sexual intercourse becomes a means for them to be holy. Just like any other action or event in their life as a married couple, they can offer this one to God. Thus, whether they derive pleasure from it or not, the marital act will be for them another opportunity to participate

[9] *Christ is Passing By* no. 24.

in Christ's Redemption, which is man's collaboration with the divine plan.

On the human level, husband and wife are well-advised to delicately ensure mutual sexual satisfaction. For the sake of one's spouse, one will sometimes have to overcome laziness, physical tiredness or boredom, as well as an uncurbed appetite for pleasure that makes one inconsiderate of the physical condition, preferences, or momentary needs of one's spouse. Uncorrected omissions or selfishness in the sexual sphere affect a person in a particularly intimate way, and this can cause serious breakdowns in other areas of the marital relationship. It is therefore important for the spouses to be sexually attuned to each other. They must know how to be "givers" and not just "takers." They must not regard sex as a mere instrument of pleasure or look at their partner as an object programmed to cater to their whims.

Likewise, married couples must take into account that men and women ordinarily have marked differences in sexual drive. In a woman, the process of sexual stimulation is slow and gradual. She can even forego full sexual satisfaction provided she enjoys her husband's warmth and affection in family life.[10] A good husband should know how to win his wife during the performance of the sexual act by appropriately giving her other words and gestures of love, the way he would at other moments of the day. The caresses, kisses and embraces which ultimately lead to the marital act must always be spurred by his pure and lasting love for his wife. A good wife, on the other hand, should not simply remain passive and on the receiving end. She, too, must spontaneously express herself and offer her husband all her feminine beauty and tenderness. Both husband and wife should be fully aware of the sanctity of the marriage bed. It must always serve as a means to grow in mutual love. And it should be kept pure on account of the great reverence they bear for the sacrament that blessed their union.

[10] "Sexual excitement rises and ebbs more gradually in women than in men. The husband therefore has the duty to moderate his sexual drive with adequate demonstrations of affection in order to synchronize himself with his wife in this respect. Otherwise, his wife, in all likelihood, will not feel satisfied and will come to regard the conjugal act as bothersome, unbecoming, and pointless, when in fact, 'The actions in marriage by which the couple are united intimately and chastely are noble and worthy ones. Expressed in a manner which is truly human, these actions promote that mutual self-giving by which spouses enrich each other with a joyful and a ready will." (Vatican Council II, Const. GS 49). Related to this is the fact that a woman does not find it too difficult to forego complete sexual satisfaction if she finds the affection she needs from her husband, and is able, in turn, to express her affection for him. These same demonstrations of affection, however, which for a woman serve to compensate for the satisfaction she may fail to get from the performance of the marital act, has a different effect for a man: instead of tempering the sexual drive in him, they only stimulate it and act as a preparatory stage for the conjugal union. Couples should always bear this in mind so that when circumstances call for conjugal continence, they will find themselves better prepared to cope with this situation. Jose Luis Soria, *Responsible Parenthood*, Madrid, 1971, 28-29.

Emotional Love

"He no longer treats me the way he used to before we got married." This is the usual complaint when details of affection are neglected. Small gestures of mutual affection matter a lot in a marriage. Little things done for love make the home a haven of peace and joy; and the human heart, being what it is, needs these expressions of love. It is always gratifying to know that one is loved and esteemed. Spouses must therefore try to show their affection for each other in various ways: a caress, a little gift, a timely phone call, a word of encouragement or comfort, or a kind remark about one's parents. These apparently trivial acts are so valuable to deepen unity and love in married life.

Still, we must highlight this: never leave off treating each other with courtesy and refinement. Many couples affirm that this is the key to a happy marriage. To be refined is to foster at every instant a deep respect—close to veneration—for one's spouse. This moves spouses to show each other every mark of kindness with utmost spontaneity but without being obsequious or servile. It means being more considerate and attune to each other's needs; it means keen-sightedness, sensitivity, confidence and simplicity; the desire to serve but without being obtrusive; and modesty that shuns prudery. In short, refinement means respect and consideration in word and in deed.

- Don't command. Suggest.
- Don't demand. Request.
- Don't assume or take things for granted. This confuses people.

- Do listen with attention and interest.
- Do smile even when things hurt.
- Do know when to keep quiet and when to speak up.
- Do respect each other's private moments.
- Never criticize the other to the face.
- Never be sarcastic.
- Never shout to make a point.
- Never use vulgar language.
- Never omit details that you know would please the other.
- Never demand for the marital act when one's spouse cannot respond due to extreme tiredness, illness or, in the case of the wife, when she has her monthly period.
- Always compliment a new outfit, a tasty dish, or a clever idea.
- Always respect one another's opinions.
- Always offer a timely word or gesture of affection.

Many more things may come to mind. It is a question of avoiding coarse and boorish manners and humiliating remarks. It means being kind and attentive and not making the other think you have more important things to do. It means the struggle to quickly get over a bad mood. But this requires generosity, self-control, humility, and a spirit of sacrifice and simplicity. It is the narrow road that leads to happiness and peace. Above all, it is the way to holiness, which is what really matters in the end. Remember, marriage is a path to sanctity. It is the road that Christian spouses follow in order to fully respond to God's invitation to all the baptized faithful: *Be perfect as your heavenly father is perfect.*

Spiritual Love

Having considered conjugal love in its sexual and affective dimensions, we shall now look into a third aspect, which involves the union of mind and heart. Married couples must try to share common principles and ideals in life, as well as common goals that they can attain together. If they want to be happy and to make each other happy, then each one must learn to make the other's aspirations his (or her) own and to transform these into a common pool of resources. It is sometimes difficult to achieve this harmony but one can always try to respect what one cannot understand and understand what one cannot share.

Spouses soon come to know each other so well that they take delight in each other's virtues and learn to accept and bear with each other's defects. They ought to learn this from the very start. It would be wrong to impose one's ways, tastes or habits on the other. If there is genuine love between them, they will try to complement each other by not focusing on the bad points of the other or harping on their differences and so end up annoying each other. If there is good will, then personal differences will never get in the way of their need to be united.

It is good for spouses to count on the fact that "although disagreements and difficulties will crop up throughout their lives, if they are solved with naturalness, they can even contribute to deepening their love. Each of us has his own character, his personal tastes, his moods—at times, his bad moods—and his defects. But we all have likeable aspects in our personality as well and for this reason and many others, everyone can be loved. It is possible to live happily together when everyone tries to correct his own defects and makes an effort to overlook the faults of others. That is to say, when there is love which cancels out and overcomes everything that might seem to be a motive for coldness or disagreement. On the other hand, if husband and wife dramatize their little differences and reproach each other for their defects and mistakes, they put an end to peace and run the risk of killing their love."[11]

Spiritual unity between husband and wife is fostered in many ways:

- Try to understand your spouse from "within"; don't stop at judging him or her from "without."
- Put yourself in his or her shoes; look at a situation from his or her perspective.
- Make it a habit to be positive in looking at and in talking about things.
- Be patient.
- Be humble. Admit a mistake. Look for the first chance to make up for it.
- Never think that you are always right because you seldom really are.
- Don't take yourself too seriously. Learn to laugh at yourself.
- Don't argue over trifles.
- Respect each other's freedom of opinion.
- Don't compete over preferences in food, entertainment, or the like.
- Don't impose your views in a bullheaded way.
- Thresh out problems in an open, friendly dialogue.

[11] *Conversations...* no. 108.

Various studies, journals and specialty publications agree that the high incidence of violence and drug addiction among the youth and many other problems have roots in homes bereft of love and understanding. This may be a hasty generalization and may not explain all the problems of the young, nevertheless it is worth dwelling on because it reflects the sad truth that many families suffer from estrangement. Husband and wife no longer talk to each other and parents hardly dialogue with their children. In these so-called dysfunctional families, aversion and mistrust reign in place of love and harmony.

When one comes down to it, such problems are often due to easily identifiable causes: husband and wife squabble over differences that they once ignored and could have dealt with before they got married. These little issues, aggravated by tiredness, selfish attitudes and lack of communication, now put a strain on their relationship. When two people have long shared a life under the same roof, it is easy to understand how and why trivial matters can be blown up. Imagine a person, who is disorderly by nature, married to someone who gets finicky about tidiness. Or one who goes for food, décor or friends that the other detests. Or a night person married to an early-riser. Or a passionate and amorous person married to a cold and passive partner. But a "perfect" couple is rare breed. There will always be certain qualities one would have wished to find in the other and certain defects that one would like to correct. After all, we are human and, therefore, far from perfect.

A point that is perhaps easily forgotten when one starts to analyze these differences in behavior and reactions is that husband and wife are not of the same sex. Many character traits of one sex that look like defects to the other are not defects at all: Women react to things the way they do simply because they are women; and men act the way they do simply because they are men. This, of course, hardly makes one sex better than the other. Men and women are simply not the same.[12] A woman may complain about things that seem ridiculous to a man. For example, she may feel hurt because her husband did not compliment her new hairdo or because he did not notice her new flower arrangement. She may get upset because he failed to thank her for cleaning up his closet or because he forgot to greet her on her birthday or on their wedding anniversary. By temperament, women give much importance to small tokens of affection or gratitude and they can feel terribly upset when these are neglected. By contrast, a man can get irritated by matters which a woman may think silly: "She did not laugh at my joke" or "She did not listen to me when I wanted to tell her something." A man can also get annoyed if his wife or children interrupt his reading or if things do not go "his way" at home. Similarly, news

[12] "A woman gives more importance to appearances and details. She is also quick to appreciate the intention behind a small gesture of affection. Small things that may seem trivial when taken alone can mean a lot to a woman because of the concern and attention that they imply. This explains why whenever the distinctive features of male and female psychologies are overlooked, the husband ends up saying his wife is wearisome because he thinks she is very sentimental and complicated. On the other hand, the wife replies by saying that her husband is boorish, inconsiderate and lacking in affection." Jose Luis Soria, *op. cit.*, 28.

that will delight a woman will hardly make a man smile. Domestic problems that could make a woman lose sleep may look like nonsense to a man.

They say that men use their head more. They approach things in a more logical way; they immediately go to the essence of a problem and do not bother about the details. On the other hand, feminine logic seems to rely more on intuition and feelings. A woman gives more importance to feelings, impressions and concrete things; they are greatly affected by the ups and downs of moods and emotions.[13] The characteristic features of men and women frequently bring corresponding defects. Thus women, for example, are easily given to jealous fits; they tend to be vain and superficial because of the preponderant role of the imagination in their psychological makeup. Men, on the other hand, can easily show brusqueness, coldness and indifference. Pride

---

[13] "An ironic remark, an attitude of indifference or coldness, an argument, a reproach, a slight injustice or simple oversight can deeply hurt a woman. A woman is gifted with wonderful resources to express her joy, sorrow and sadness in many ways. Her imagination and memory are highly sensitive to beauty and this enables her to express her delicate love with all the warmth of her feminine charm. Her intuitions can also be very penetrating. On the other hand, this keen inner sensitivity, which accounts for much of her ingenuity and affective charm, at the same time colors her whole outlook towards life. A woman, for instance, can take great delight in small tokens of affection. Her decisions and attitudes also tend to be deeply affected by last impressions unless special effort is exerted to view things in a broader, more objective way. Similarly, her idea of love usually evokes demonstrations of tender care and the joys of a home more than anything else; she seeks to be pampered, protected and lavished with affection." Jose M. Ardions, *Marriages on the Edge*, *Palabra* Magazine, 48-49, 1964.

can bring them to be inconsiderate with women. Moreover, because of their habit of looking at the logical side of any problem, they think they are always right.

Experts have come up with various studies on how men and women differ in psychological makeup and they generally agree on the basics. Without implying that one sex is superior to the other, they associate strength, creativity, action and reason with men, while they attribute keen intuition and a high emotive capacity and sensitivity to women. Men, they say, tend to be unstable in loving while women are endowed with a greater capacity to be faithful.[14]

[14] "As regards the capacity to love, a man can be likened to a raging stream that is soon at rest once absorbed in the sea of professional and social commitments. A woman, by contrast, is like a silent brook whose steady flow reflects the untiring attention she affords her beloved. Man is like a heavy but passing rain shower, while woman is like the steadfast earth— Mother Earth, as poets are wont to say. The former, a being of action, the latter, an object of contemplation. Woman offers tenderness, refuge and tender consolation to man's wounded pride. She is also there to check his headlong rush into the fast pace of life. Man invents and breaks frontiers, woman preserves tradition. Mothers are never revolutionaries, but conservatives, the source of social stability. A man will give direct orders to have his way; woman gets hers by subtly weaving in and out the sinuous footpaths of feelings, where the forthright habits of men lose battles. Sensitivity is woman's weakness; pride is man's. Thus in the game of love woman usually gets even by attacking the pride of her man. Before she gives herself to him, woman demands his support. For that sense of security, she pledges to him her tenderness and understanding. And she will reciprocate his love by leaving herself completely in his hands. It is a woman's deep affective nature that accounts for all this. This explains her constancy in love and in adversity, as well as her tendency to jealous possessiveness." Jaime Fernandez, *Love and Sexuality*, Madrid, 24-26.

Such differences can seriously strain conjugal relations if they are overlooked and not assessed with calm objectivity. However, they can also be harnessed so that husband and wife can actually live in harmony because they realize that they complement each other. Think about it for a while and see how God created man so unlike a woman precisely because he wanted their mutual integration in marriage. And from this mutual integration shall spring a complete being endowed with the qualities that nature had given man and woman separately. The two indeed have become one flesh once they achieve their goal of spiritual unity. And once a couple decides to constantly work at it together, nothing can break them apart. Note that the key is to work at it with constancy, at the first sign of a rupture or even if the damage seems beyond repair.

This is why husband and wife must always try to reconcile their differences. They must know how to "give in" because this is part of the effort of mutual self-giving. They must also accept each other's defects and idiosyncrasies, combining this with the constant readiness to forgive and the willingness to help each other overcome their faults. At the same time, they must be aware that many defects take more than a few days to correct; some, in fact, will take a lifetime to change. Spiritual union is difficult to achieve but it is transcendent to pursue it with an upright, humble, patient, sincere and self-sacrificing attitude. A whole series of virtues come into play when spouses strive to be spiritually united. In the process, they radiate peace and harmony in the home. Of course, this attitude entails a deep respect for each other's freedom and personality. It also means mutual respect for and acceptance of their perceptions and attitudes towards the world.

The human joy that comes with conjugal unity is a powerful incentive for spouses to work untiringly for it. Yet there remains one more motive, which is the most sublime of all. The love of God and the desire to be holy and to live the Christian ideal ought to spur them on. When other reasons fail, spouses must engrave in their hearts the supernatural reasons that should move them to recover a love that seems lost or to fix one that seems to be at breaking point. They must remember that marriage is a divine call, a vocation, and that they can count on the sacramental nature of the bond that unites them in prayer and generous sacrifice.

Supernatural Love

The Holy Spirit, infused in the sacramental celebration of Matrimony, offers Christian spouses a gift of a new communion of love, which is the living and real image of the most singular unity of the Church, the undivided Mystical Body of Jesus Christ. This new dimension of love allows the married couple to participate in God's love through the supernatural virtue of charity which, by supernatural grace, is infused into the human heart.

In this regard, St Paul addressed the Colossians and all Christians in a text that the Church incorporated into the liturgy of the Feast of the Holy Family:

Put on then, as God's chosen ones, holy and beloved, compassion, kindness, lowliness, meekness, and patience, forbearing one another and, if one has a complaint against another, forgiving each other; as the Lord has forgiven you, so you also must forgive ... Wives, be subject to your husbands, as is fitting in the Lord. Husbands, love your wives and do not be harsh with them. Children, obey your parents in everything, for this pleases the Lord. Fathers, do not provoke your children, lest they become discouraged.[15]

The love of God is the ultimate reference point of the unity of husband and wife. Supernatural charity guides a Christian's relations with all men, most especially with those one is closest to. God's love will move the spouses to support each other, to make sacrifices for each other and to always walk through life together along the road of fidelity. By the power of this theological virtue, a man and a woman who are blessed with the sacrament of Matrimony lead a life of mutual self-giving and dedication which is so satisfying that they feel blessed emptying themselves for the good of the other.

The grace of the married state is a definitive element in Christian marriage. It acts unhindered through time and makes the joys and challenges of married life fruitful. Of course, this grace has to grow and take deep roots. It is therefore the spouses' duty to cultivate it in their spiritual life, that is, through their relationship with God and by striving to grow in faith, hope and charity. Many problems of whatever magnitude and sort are resolved in and through prayer. This means that the couple considers the matter in God's presence and reflects on it in the light of the faith, the way God sees it. A life of prayer produces lasting peace

[15] Col 3:12-13; 18-21.

and serenity, as well as the great joy of knowing that one's marriage is not only bearing temporary fruit: it has become a true path to personal holiness and a magnificent instrument to lead other souls to God.

As a consequence, the home is the primary place for a person to practice and fulfill God's basic commandment: *You shall love the Lord your God with all your heart, and with all your soul, and with all your mind. This is the great and first commandment. And a second is like it, You shall love your neighbor as yourself.*[16] Divine love intertwines with and elevates the love for one's husband, wife, and children. Thus human love raised to the supernatural order is capable of fusing two distinct persons into one. A married couple once said that they are so different that they always look at the world through opposite windows. "Still," they affirmed, "there is something that has united us in our 30 years of marriage. It is the love of God. This has kept us united and it has always helped us to struggle and overcome our differences."

Love, from the supernatural perspective, is charity built on kindness and mutual respect, forgiveness, tenderness, and an understanding smile. The spouses forget themselves and are constantly seeking that which would please the other, and the joy of sharing one life and one goal: the glory of God and to be holy and to live charity and the other supernatural virtues in the married state.

"They will achieve this aim by exercising the virtues of faith and hope, serenely facing all the great and small problems which confront any family, and

---

[16] Mt 22:37-39.

persevering in the love and enthusiasm with which they fulfill their duties. In this way they practice the virtue of charity in all things. They learn to smile and forget about themselves in order to pay attention to others. Husband and wife will listen to each other and to their children, showing them that they are really loved and understood. They will forget about the unimportant little frictions that selfishness could magnify out of proportion. They will lovingly do all the small acts of service that make up their daily life together."[17]

The supernatural character of love is at the heart of the dialogue with married couples. If they have no desire to be holy and if they ignore the divine transcendence of their relationship, then their marriage will only be a two-dimensional reality. It would have no depth. It could be filled with many wonderful human realities. It could be very fruitful, humanly speaking. But it would have lost the basic element, which is that Christ called the married couple for a single purpose: to love God. Of this, St Paul wrote: *If I speak in the tongues of men and of angels, but have not love, I am a noisy gong or a clanging cymbal. And if I have prophetic powers, and understand all mysteries and all knowledge, and if I have all faith, so as to remove mountains, but have not love, I am nothing. If I give away all I have, and if I deliver my body to be burned, but have not love, I gain nothing.*[18]

---

[17] *Christ is Passing By* no. 23.
[18] 1 Cor 13:1-3.

FOSTERING MUTUAL LOVE

"The love between husband and wife and, in a derivatory and broader way, the love between members of the same family—between parents and children, brothers and sisters and relatives and members of the household—is given life and sustenance by an unceasing inner dynamism leading the family to ever deeper and more intense *communion*, which is the foundation and soul of the *community* of marriage and the family."[19]

All four dimensions of love, from the carnal to the supernatural, are intertwined and, ideally, must be present in the love of a married couple. But reality proves otherwise. Many couples lack one or two or are sorely deficient in all dimensions. In which case, a false concept of any one dimension can place the integrity of their love on the line. For example, a couple may wallow in the corporal dimension of their relationship, disregarding the spiritual dimension and even the possibility of bearing children. Theirs is a trivial, pleasure-based relationship no different from a hedonistic game, or the so-called casual sex. On the other hand, a couple with a misguided sense of spirituality can neglect or even despise the corporal dimension, resulting in a cold, disembodied union. Again, some couples place undue stress on the procreative dimension and so forget or even forego the joys that loving dialogue and mutual attention bring; they wind up being a "baby factory." Finally, a couple who meets all the other dimensions of love but neglects the spiritual-rational dimension of their relationship will

[19] *FC* 18.

find it very hard to obtain the ideal sharing of a life because they have not learned to communicate their innermost ideals, concerns and aspirations.

Some dimensions of love are less developed and not as firmly rooted than others because of man's pride and selfishness. Ours is a fallen nature and pride born of original sin is a wound that almost never heals. Nevertheless, we have a lot of hope to be better than what we are right now. Many-a marriage has been saved by simply sitting down and discussing how one dimension of the relationship can be renewed, recovered, or healed. Mutual support and a resolute struggle are enough to rekindle love in a home, but this has to be mustered with all the vigor and enthusiasm of those first years together. The goal is worth fighting for.

It is not easy to love: one has to learn to give one's self unconditionally and without setting any limits. At first, love can be an intense feeling, which is what being "in love" is all about. However, a couple will only love each other truly after a long process of personal maturation. The wedding day is just the beginning of this lifelong process and euphoric starts do not maintain the primary inertia. Real love demands constant progress and continued self-mastery. In this lies its greatness. One cannot fall into routine: it's either you climb higher or you slide back. Love can easily grow cold, and love that grows cold kills happiness and, almost readily, faithfulness. "Marriage is a process of development and transformation. When a person does not get into the process, one's marriage will always be in danger and will always be beset with problems. A real and total encounter does not happen overnight, not even in two or three years of being together."[20]

When a couple get married, they commit themselves to grow in love. The honeymoon phase may find them with the lively determination never to turn their backs on each other, come what may. But getting a headstart is easy; what matters is to cross the finish line. Problems and sorrows will never be lacking, but these do not endanger but rather reinforce and confirm love. Shared sacrifice unites people in a profound way.

Love is like a fragile plant left out in the open and which must be carefully cultivated so that it may slowly grow and reach full and healthy maturity. One has to take care of love the way a good gardener maintains his best roses. He fertilizes the soil and prunes the branches. He gets worried when a plant rots or looses its petals and immediately takes pains to cure it. He is enraptured by the beauty of his blossoms and feels a part of himself go with the death of every plant. Now, what would two persons in love not do to keep their relationship alive and happy? How could they watch their source of real physical and spiritual fulfillment die? It would be gravely irresponsible to do so. Rather, they exert all effort to develop and strengthen their love and to protect it from all danger.

FIGHT FOR IT!

The first thing to do to defend one's love is to avoid anything that can anger or annoy one or the other spouse. Annoyances may come in words, attitudes,

[20] Ardions, José, *op. cit.*

shortcomings, or personality quirks. Be sensitive to small symptoms of coldness or isolation. Love cools down slowly. The process is hardly discernible at the start, and the couple realizes it only when serious conflicts arise and the remedies are hard to find. Hence, be keen in catching those trivial things and incidents that can bring about devastating consequences.

Trouble sometimes begins when the husband starts coming home late from work. His job may really call for it, but he may also have that notion that family duties are limited to weekends. Then again, this could be a symptom of waning interest in his wife and children. He may have grown weary of the simple joys of coming home, or the light in his children's eyes when he spends some time playing with them or taking them out for a walk or answering their countless questions about life. On the other hand, it could be the wife's fault. She has probably lost interest in winning him. She goes about cold or grouchy, sad-faced and slovenly. Worse, she may not even be home to meet him. Perhaps she has become neglectful of the food at table, the household chores, and the cleanliness of the home.

Some years back, the US Gallup Poll classified men's more common complaints about their wives:

- She bickers and nags.
- She never gives a word of encouragement or praise.
- She spends too much.
- She's never at home and goes out for no good reason.
- She neglects the house and the kids;
- She's nosy.

- She's a gossip.
- She's a chronic faultfinder.
- She has a lot of gripes and hang-ups.
- She's such a grouch.
- She tells lies.
- She makes mountains out of molehills.
- She's always late.
- She takes too long dressing up when we go out on a date.
- She's too bossy.
- She's a slob. She never dresses up the way she used to before we got married.

Wives ought to examine this list because it often explains why their husbands suddenly become cold and indifferent to them.

The Gallup Poll also enumerates the more frequent complaints wives have about their husbands:

- He's always out with the boys.
- His meetings run till late at night (The No. 1 complaint in the list. She feels abandoned and lonely when this happens. She thinks it unfair that he should leave the entire burden of the home on her.)
- He takes me for granted, now that I am not as young and as attractive as before. He flirts with younger women.
- He only thinks of himself.
- He's bossy and domineering.
- He's like a baby when he's sick.
- He's a tightwad with me but spends a lot on himself.

- He doesn't take on his share in the home and in bringing up the kids. He thinks this is women's stuff.
- He's a workaholic. He has no time for me. He's not at home when we need him. We never go out.

Husband and wife must frequently think and talk about these issues in a free-flowing and uninterrupted dialogue. The worst thing that can happen to a married couple is that they stop speaking to each other. Whatever happens, they must talk and get to the bottom of each other's thoughts, feelings and impressions. Spouses must try to understand how each one feels and learn to apologize for hurt feelings. In the same light, they ought to firmly set aside grudges and the urge to "get even." John Paul II acknowledges that it is difficult to erase some painful memories as these are like deep and fresh wounds in the hearts of the spouses.

Nevertheless, "The love of spouses and parents has the capacity to cure these kinds of wounds, provided the dangers alluded to do not deprive it of its regenerative force, which is so beneficial and wholesome a thing for human communities. This capacity depends on the divine grace of forgiveness and reconciliation, which always ensures the spiritual energy to begin anew. For this very reason family members need to encounter Christ in the Church through the wonderful Sacrament of Penance and Reconciliation.

In this context, we can realize how important prayer is with families and for families, in particular for those threatened by division. We need to pray that married couples will love their vocation, even when the road becomes difficult, or the paths become narrow, uphill and seemingly insuperable; we need to pray that, even then, they will be faithful to their covenant with God."[21]

Problems that can endanger the constancy of love can never cause a couple to throw family stability out the window, along with the love on which it is built. On the contrary, difficulties and the struggle to overcome them should reinforce their love.

MAKE IT GROW

In another homily, John Paul II emphasizes that couples have assumed the serious commitment and the grave obligation to nourish their love for the sake of their union and for the stability of their home. It is a mistake to be happy just "getting by." This is why couples who value this treasure do not stop at "guarding" their love from harm: They foster a constant and positive attitude to make it better. Think on your own and together, as a couple. What more can we do to enrich our marriage?

It would be good to pray about it and to ask the Holy Spirit for specific guidance and inspiration. The answer may be this: Work at affective integration, the sharing of ideals. Shared ideals sustain and develop love. The wife must take interest in her husband's job, and the husband, in the concerns of the home. He should remember to bring her flowers or chocolates on important anniversaries, while she must take pains to look good for him when he comes home at the end of

[21] John Paul II, *Letter to Families*, 2 February 1994, no. 14.

the day. These details are a surefire way of keeping love and fidelity living and vibrant.

Regarding this, Saint Josemaría Escrivá wrote: "As long as we walk on this earth, suffering will always be the touchstone of love. If we were to describe what occurs in the married state, we could say that there are two sides to the coin. On the one hand, there is the joy of knowing that one is loved, the desire and enthusiasm involved in starting a family and taking care of it, the love of husband and wife, the happiness of seeing the children grow up. On the other hand, there are also sorrows and difficulties—the passing of time that consumes the body and threaten the character with the temptation to bitterness, the seemingly monotonous succession of days that are apparently always the same.

We would have a poor idea of marriage and of human affection if we were to think that love and joy come to an end when faced with such difficulties. It is precisely then that our true sentiments come to the surface. Then the tenderness of a person's gift of himself takes root and show itself in a true and profound affection that is stronger than death (*Cf. Song of Solomon 8:6*)."[22]

To summarize, married couples who want to work at achieving maximum perfection in their love can bear in mind two things: be ready to give without expecting anything in return and learn to fall in love with each other again.

[22] *Christ is Passing By* no. 24.

THE ART OF GIVING

Marriage is human love's endeavor to seek earthly happiness and, through it, arrive at a final encounter with Divine Love. This is why mutual generosity is intrinsic to marital life. To love is to give one's self and to give up selfishness and comfort-seeking. It is to find joy in making one's partner and family happy, being responsible to form a home that radiates warmth and happiness. This requires the spouses to do away with self love and to make the needs of the others their priority. Couples who do not constantly strive to deny themselves of personal whims and pleasures can only bring disaster upon themselves. Laziness or apathy can never be an excuse to deny the other a reasonable request, no matter how small or insignificant it may seem. Each one must positively and actively work at seeking what is good and pleasing to the other, which is the secret behind every bright and cheerful home.

This is why a person will never be happy or be capable of giving happiness if he remains selfish, short-sighted and concerned solely about his comfort. Spouses must be ready to give without reserve if they want their marriage to work. Conjugal love ought to model itself after the very love of Christ, who emptied himself for the Church and for each one of us...*a fragrant offering pleasing to God* (Eph 4:18).[23]

---

[23] Cf. John Paul II, *Homily*, 8 April 1987.

FALLING IN LOVE AGAIN

Complacency endangers fidelity and constancy in love. Being too confident that one's spouse will never leave him or her leads to neglect, which stunts and even kills love. This is why spouses must try to win each other and to fall in love again every day. To reawaken love in all its dimensions is a great challenge for spouses and signifies spiritual, affective and sexual growth in daily living. A wife, for instance, can continually charm her husband by taking care of her looks and her grooming. She has to try to look as young and as attractive as before while maintaining a certain air of flirtatiousness, mystery and surprise that would captivate and enthrall her husband.[24]

Other pointers:

- Take positive interest in his professional concerns, hobbies and sports, but don't be prying or meddlesome. Avoid asking impertinent questions. Learn when to give a sensible opinion and when to keep timely and discreet silence.
- Be concerned about his health.
- Don't be jealous of his professional or social life.
- Never go to bed upset with each other. Smile when you get up the next day.
- Help him cut on expenses, especially on luxury items or services.
- Be more than interested in befriending his family and friends but without sacrificing the attention due to your home. Such is the hierarchy of love.

All this may be a difficult but worthy investment because it is the family's happiness, now and in the future, which is at stake. Moreover, when you reach the twilight years, you will be able to reap wonderful fruit from what you had generously sown in the springtime of your love.

Owing to her psychological bent, the woman usually bears the bulk of the job, but she must never think that this is exclusively a woman's job. Husbands, too, must take note because in this lies the secret of love's eternal youth:

[24] In an interview for the women's magazine, TELVA, the Founder of Opus Dei, St Josemaria Escrivá was asked: "What would you tell a married woman so that she may lead a happy and exciting life? This question may seem trivial but our magazine receives many letters from readers who are interested in this topic." He answered: "I think it's a very important question and the answers are just as important. For a marriage to be continually exciting, the wife must try to win her husband every day, and the husband, his wife. They can renew their love each time through sacrifice and also with a smile and a dash of naughtiness. If the husband comes home tired from work, and his wife starts to talk endlessly about what went wrong that day, don't be surprised that he'd lose his patience. Unpleasant matters can be set aside for a better moment when he's more relaxed and ready to listen. Another detail: take care of your personal grooming. If another priest says otherwise, I think he's giving bad advice. The older one gets, the more she should try to look better, not just spiritually, but also and precisely, physically—though she must do so in a way that suits her age and social standing. I usually say this as a joke, but the older the façade of a house, the more it needs repainting. This is a priest's advice. A traditional Spanish saying goes: A beautiful wife keeps her husband away from other doors. This is why I dare say that women are to be blamed 80% of the time if their husbands go astray: they do not know how to win them each day. They do not know how to offer them pleasing, refined details of affection."

- You, too, must never neglect your looks.
- Give importance to the tiny details that mean a lot to your wife, like thanking her for polishing your shoes or for serving your favorite snack when you least expected it.
- Remember important dates, like when you got engaged, your wedding anniversary, her birthday, or her parents' wedding anniversary. The memory may fail but a good diary with a perpetual calendar should come in handy.
- Remember how you first met; what you said to each other and what you did; the movies you used to watch, and the music you used to listen to. A couple who collects pleasant memories brings warmth and cheer to the home.
- Always be very affectionate and tender to her. Second-guess her innermost thoughts and desires.
- Respond to her need to be loved as well as to her legitimate sexual desires, even if sometimes this would entail effort and sacrifice. Your attention counts more than any expensive gift or trip that you can get to compensate for the lack of affection.

A husband who acts this way is easily more loveable to his wife and their home will retain the freshness of their first love.

However, as the head of the family, a husband must combine tenderness with strength, drive and initiative. A woman seeks a strong and virile partner to complement her feminine sensibility and need for support. A husband's support must be real, felt and unstinting. He has to show her that she is more important than his work or his buddies. This will move her to take interest in his professional and financial concerns. But he must try to show a measure of confidence and control to spare her unnecessary worries.

"A wife is not only meant to give physical companionship to her husband; her presence must be felt in every sphere of his life. A true wife is not only interested in some of the problems of her husband; since she loves him completely, she must want to share in all his concerns. It is in this way that a woman lives up to her God-given role of being the 'other half' of her husband's life."[25]

Ordinarily, spouses want to—and even have the right to—participate in the life of the other, even if one does not understand much of, say, the other's job. And so even if the wife is not at all interested in her husband's professional field, she still sees it as a chance to penetrate his inner world more deeply. A prudent and loving spouse will ask for advise and help from the other who, in turn, should try to listen attentively and offer sensible solutions. And even if one decides to follow a different course of action, it is always advisable to show appreciation and to take seriously the other's opinion. Nothing can be more hurtful than to have one's ideas rejected, be it in public or in the privacy of the bedroom.

If husband and wife behave in this way, their union not only will preserve its strength and freshness, but will also become a source of inspiration and comfort for the spouses, the children, and the people

[25] Gertrud von le Fort, *The Eternal Woman*, Rialp, Madrid, 1957, 99-100.

who, in one way or another, take part in the family's daily encounters. This is what living the fullness of Christian life in marriage is all about.

A loving wife, a cheerful and self-sacrificing mother who makes life easy for her husband and opens new horizons to her children will always communicate joy and hope. And even when she grows old and loses her youthful good looks, she will have won forever the heart of her husband. In his eyes, she will be the only woman in his life—the mother of his children and his irreplaceable companion in youth and in old age. Likewise, when the husband would have lost his health and vitality and his capacity for work, his wife will continue looking up to him as her lifetime companion and support. He will always have her unfailing love and admiration.

A tender and unwavering fidelity is therefore the foundation of married love in old age. This entails constant effort to generously live all the facets of conjugal love, from the physical to the supernatural. And when the children shall have left home, life goes on for the senior couple, now bent with the weight of years, but still united and happy because they are savoring the human and supernatural fruits of their fidelity. Nothing can be more beautiful than the sound of an elderly lady's trembling voice that still brings light to her aging husband's eyes. Perhaps he can no longer move his hand to caress her face but he is moved contemplating the woman with whom he had enjoyed the joys and sorrows of a lifetime.

GETTING TO SPECIFICS

The physical dimension

- Be sensitive to what pleases your partner sexually. Harmonize your needs.
- Know the intimate desires of the other.
- Don't rush into the act. Make sure you ease yourselves into it with the indispensable words and gestures of tenderness.
- Never deny your partner out of selfishness, comfort, laziness or spite.
- Never be passive or bored.
- Take care of your looks and your grooming. Try to keep physically trim and in good shape. Go on a diet and exercise if you have to.
- Be spontaneous. Resorting to artificial gadgets and pornographic films take away the intimacy and candor of the sexual act.

The affective dimension

- Foster affection. Romance, which can be giddy and immature at the start, fades with time. Shower each other with loving smiles, words, touches, and other affectionate gestures.
- Learn to empathize, that is, to validate and echo each other's feelings of joy, sadness, or pain. One can lose this capacity when one gets too immersed in one's problems and concerns.
- Be perceptive of the other's weak points. Learn

to catch what worries the other. It could be the fear of loneliness or of excessive control.

- Know how to please one another. Wear the outfit he or she likes to see you in. Keep each other company watching his or her favorite TV show.
- Be the best of friends. Look at your spouse as a person and get interested in his or her life, preferences, desires, ambitions and joys. Share intimacies. Talk about a wide array of topics.
- Be a good companion. Do things that you enjoy together: going to the movies, watching a play, taking a stroll or playing some sports.

The spiritual dimension

- Work at achieving common ideals. If you have not reached this point, then support each other's goals and aspirations.
- Agree on basic principles on how to obtain your individual life goals and those of your children. When this is not possible due to culture, race or religion, then identify points of convergence. Work on these, while respecting those in which you differ.
- Define basic goals that you can achieve as a couple.
- Understand each other. Accept each other for what one is and not for how you want him or her to be.
- Be interested in anything that would make the other happy.
- Make each other feel and know, in words and

actions, that he or she is the most important person in your life.

- Support and encourage each other especially in moments of discouragement or uncertainty.
- Take time to talk about common domestic concerns: the children, the house, the finances, possible investments, and expenses.
- Respect each other's opinion. Don't impose your point of view.
- Don't meddle in matters that do not directly concern you and which you have nothing definitive to say about, like the concerns of your spouse's colleagues, friends, and relatives.

The supernatural dimension

- Face difficulties and problems calmly and with supernatural sense.
- Fight routine or boredom in fulfilling your duties toward spouse and children.
- Forget about yourself. Think of what you can do to make the others happy.
- Help each other be holy by praying for one another.
- Abandon family concerns into the hands of God.
- Bear the ups and downs of daily living with a cheerful attitude.
- Understand each other without reserve or restrictions.
- Be forgiving, always.
- Never neglect constant and devout prayer.

DEALING WITH MARRIAGE ON THE ROCKS

It is a common and natural thing for people to quarrel. Siblings do, parents and children do, and likewise friends and co-workers. Owe this to the myriad of ever-changing circumstances and to differences in character, upbringing and life philosophy. Small wonder that fights should be more frequent among persons living under the same roof. They are in a situation where it is easier to find more things and reasons to argue about. In the case of married couples, one has to add such factors as the intimate sharing of an entire life and their being so familiar with each another's deep-seated faults and limitations. Remember, too, the basic psychological differences between men and women. On the whole, there is no reason to get surprised or obsessed about the matter. It is a challenge for husband and wife to avoid disagreements, large or small, from piling up to breaking point. In this section, however, we want focus on extreme situations that can actually make a couple opt for separation as the only way out for them and for their children.

POSSIBLE REASONS

Infidelity

Extra-marital affairs damage affectivity in marriage. These put a crack on the foundations of fidelity. Such relations may be carnal or sentimental; they can begin with momentary flirtation or a one-time fling that takes on a serious turn and eventually goes out of control.

Infidelity poisons love. One cannot think, "What you don't know won't hurt you." Infidelity is always a grave deception of the love and loyalty of one's spouse and children. A thousand reasons can never justify it. If you are cheating on your partner or are just about to, think again. Bring to mind the many reasons to immediately get out of this situation.

Alcoholism or drug addiction

Unfortunately, this is a common reason. Many times, the alcoholic or drug addict will never admit being "hooked." One argues that he can quit anytime and so refuses to seek help. The sane spouse and the children will eventually get fed up and probably decide to throw him out of the house. If the alcoholic or drug addict sincerely wants to change, he must first admit it, even at the very first stages, and seek adequate therapy before the home falls apart.

An ill or unstable character

One can put up with a person who is irascible, excessively intolerant, shrewish, suspicious, or domineering only for a time. Even the most patient person has limits.

Boorishness. Physical or verbal abuse

This can be the consequence of alcoholism, drug addiction or of an ill or unstable character. Domestic violence degrades family life. It blinds both perpetrator and victims and can soon end a marriage.

Money Matters

When a family is in financial straits, quarrels can arise especially when the couple does not face matters calmly, patiently and with supernatural sense and detachment. In a family problem such as this, everyone should pitch in by tightening their belts. Complaining does not help. This is a sensitive situation and the pressure can unleash a major conflict.

Then again, there is the problem of differing attitudes toward administering family properties. Husband and wife must realize that they are equally responsible in managing their property. As a consequence, they enjoy equal rights to decide on major or minor expenses as well as on the distribution of the goods acquired, down to the shoes and clothes of the children. They must come to an agreement in this area so as to avoid unnecessary complaints in the future.

Finally, financial irresponsibility. The husband is usually faulted for this because he is expected to be the breadwinner of the house. A man who tends to be a slacker seriously disappoints his wife and risks losing her respect for him. Not that she totally loses interest in him, but her feminine makeup seeks security in all aspects, most especially when it comes to earning the money needed to get on with life and to dutifully feed and educate their children.

Unequal responsibility in bringing up the children

The husband plays an indispensable role in raising the children. He therefore must look into it with due dedication and responsibility and not delegate it solely to his wife. Spouses share in the task of forming their children. This is why parents who spend too much time in the office run the risk of gradually losing their children's trust and affection. However, most of the time, it is the mother who attends PTA meetings, which may show the father's lack of concern in this area. He cannot cite work as an excuse because there is no business more important and more urgent than the proper education of the children. The husband must realize that he cannot keep on passing the buck to his wife; he also risks losing her respect in this regard.[26] To understand this is a sign of maturity and averts serious marital conflicts.

Sexual and affective incompatibility

To avoid repetition, we refer to the subheadings "Physical Love," "Affective Love," "Fight for It" and "Let It Grow," which exhaustively deal with these topics.

[26] J. Abad and E. Fenoy, *Children*, Sinag-tala Publishers, Ch. 2.

An unhealthy attachment to one's blood family

The following symptoms point to an excessive and disorderly dedication and attachment to one's blood family:

- using family funds to help out one's relatives without consulting or, despite the objections of, one's spouse;
- spending more time with one's relatives than with one's own family;
- allowing in-laws to meddle in the concerns of the spouses and the children (for example, family expenses, the care and décor of the home, etc.)

Such behavior triggers hostility towards one's in-laws and causes the aggrieved spouse to take it out on his or her partner. Recurring incidents in this regard can eventually cause a crisis.

An unhealthy attachment to one's work

Both husband and wife are prone to this type of "syndrome" whose main symptom is work-alcoholism. Giving excessive importance to one's work and to the concerns of the workplace, and allowing these to invade the family space can very well destroy family life and erode a marriage. Remember that the home is sacred and one's spouse and children are of top priority.

The working mother can become so taken up by her job that she forgets her basic role. She must remember that she is first a wife and a mother and that no one else can fit into her shoes—not even the best nanny or school. A workaholic wife poses a more serious problem to the home because the mother holds a unique and special influence over her family. One may blame the husband who indirectly pushes his wife to seek personal fulfillment outside the home because he neglects her needs and does not show any appreciation for the work she does at home. In other cases, it is the wife who desires to prove herself and to receive professional accolade in a corporate setup. Which is a legitimate ambition, but not to the detriment of her primary call as wife, mother and the heart of the home.

Work-alcoholism leads to a breakdown in marriage because work pressures leave the spouses no time for peaceful conversation. Before they realize it, they have become estranged and any trifle can cause an explosion.

Irreconcilable differences

We often tend to judge people and events by our own standards and personal viewpoints. As a consequence, it becomes very difficult to accept others as they are. We are prone to exaggerating other people's defects and to be very subjective in looking at and interpreting other people's intentions. Which is opposed to loving, the cordial and grateful acceptance of others as they are. "Charity consists not so much in giving as in understanding."[27] This is the only way to help a person. A person is motivated to change when he realizes that he is accepted as he is. Peaceful and harmonious living is built on mutual understanding.

[27] *The Way* no. 463.

It is then not surprising that the absence of understanding causes feelings of isolation that can build up
into a real crisis.

Lack of appreciation

The spouses can get so used to each other's good
points that they can take each other for granted. Thus
the complaint, "He is nicer to his friends than to me"
or "I never seem to do anything right." This disillusion
isolates people and makes affection grow cold. On the
other hand one can recover the warmth of affection by
praising the qualities and professional achievements
of the other. Do something about it before crisis sets in.

Coldness

As mentioned earlier, conjugal love is like a delicate
plant that must be cultivated with patience and
constancy. However, one must not be content with an
interior acknowledgment of the other's virtues or with
simply recalling pleasant memories of the kindness
and generosity of one's spouse. Affection must also be
shown through affectionate hugs and kisses, holding
hands, loving words and glances, praises, gifts, and
words of appreciation and gratitude. These may come
out spontaneously at the start but can be neglected
and even disappear as years pass. Loving gestures
and words must never be omitted because they are
necessary for the patient and constant cultivation of
love. Routine leads to cooling down, then to simply
"putting up" with each other, and, finally to a crisis.

Lack of communication

This is a common problem and the frequent cause of a crisis.

- It can happen because of an omission. One keeps quiet about something that must be said and instead resorts to withdrawal, denial or sarcasm.
- On the other hand, the defect may lie in how one receives the message: by playing deaf on purpose; by letting words flow into one ear and out the other; by being too sensitive or defensive (What are you implying?); by twisting things around (Are you blaming me for what happened last week?)
- The message itself may be imprecise, hostile, rash or reproving.
- Also take note of how the message is delivered: it could be incomplete or disrespectful, rude or said in a shouting manner.

Neglect of one's physical appearance

This applies to both the husband and the wife even if physical beauty is appreciated and expected more in a woman than in a man. A woman who lets herself grow fat and sloppy risks losing her self esteem and confidence in the face of others--her husband especially. There is another side to the coin: the husband would tend to set his sights on the prettier women around. Thus both are responsible for looking as best as they can for each other.

Pride

Man's greatest enemy is a lamentable legacy of our first parents. Pride is a capital sin that harms not only us, personally, but also everyone else who gets involved with us. Pride lies at the bottom of all marital problems and breakups. This is why we must watch out for its many subtle symptoms:

- a sickly touchiness; feeling hurt by everything and anything;
- the desire to stand out and to call attention;
- not accepting one's limitations;
- not apologizing for mistakes and refusing to make up for them;
- despising suggestions or commands;
- making excuses for a fault committed;
- being too concerned about what others may think or say of us;
- insincerity;
- refusing to be helped;
- faultfinding and openly criticizing others;[28]
- smugly talking about one's self and one's qualities and accomplishments;
- undue and excessive bossiness;
- nitpicking;
- being an unpleasant know-it-all;
- being scornful, sarcastic and acerbic;
- obsessively analyzing humiliations suffered or even one's own shortcomings and those of others;
- wanting to manipulate others;

[28] "Don't make negative criticism. If you can't praise, say nothing." *The Way* no. 443.

- thinking that we are indispensable;
- telling lies to look good to the rest of the world.

Humility is a very important virtue that one must strive to practice in order to prevent the evil that pride can wreak on one's self and on one's relationship. We must try to see and accept ourselves the way God sees and accepts us—with defects, weaknesses and limitations. We are neither impeccable nor infallible, and we can fail so many times. So why not admit it?

To be humble is also to welcome unexpected, or even unreasonable humiliation and reproof from others—that is, unless the injustice does not gravely damage one's good name or that of one's family. A humble person does not take himself or his opinions too seriously. In fact, he thinks little of himself and does not get extremely upset by what others say (or not say) about him. He's ready to overlook the shortcomings of people and prefers to remain in the background. In an argument or in discussions, he never presumes that he's always right and is open to advice and suggestions.

Humility takes a lifetime to learn.[29] To acquire it, one must regularly "pull self-love out by the roots and

[29] "Allow me to remind you that among other evident signs of a lack of humility are:

-Thinking that what you do or say is better than what others do or say;

-Always wanting to get your own way;

-Arguing when you are not right or—when you are— insisting stubbornly or with bad manners;

-Giving your opinion without being asked for it, when charity does not demand you to do so;

-Despising the point of view of others;

plant in its place love for Jesus Christ. That is the secret of effectiveness and happiness."[30]

SURVIVING A CRISIS

To save your marriage, the first step is to "want to." A marriage is well worth saving for many reasons:

- The well-being of the children. Despite all arguments, there is no doubt that children have to be raised by *both* parents and that the parents have to be *together*. Children from broken homes will never have the same psycho-emotional develop-

---

-Not being aware that all the gifts and qualities you have are on loan;

-Not acknowledging that you are unworthy of all honor or esteem, even the ground you are treading on or the things you own;

-Mentioning yourself as an example in conversation;

-Speaking badly about yourself, so that they may form a good opinion of you, or contradict you;

-Making excuses when rebuked;

-Hiding some humiliating faults from your director, so that he may not lose the good opinion he has of you;

-Hearing praise with satisfaction, or being glad that others have spoken well of you;

-Being hurt that others are held in greater esteem than you;

-Refusing to carry out menial tasks;

-Seeking or wanting to be singled out;

-Letting drop words of self-praise in conversation, or words that might show your honesty, your wit or skill, your professional prestige...;

-Being ashamed of not having certain possessions..."

St J. Escrivá, *Furrow*, no. 263.

[30] *Op. cit.*, no. 696.

ment as those raised in a stable family atmosphere. All sorts of statistics, as well as personal
experience, reflect this.

- The well-being of the spouses. Keeping the bond
of fidelity guarantees and is the foundation of
a stable and upright married life. Fidelity is the
sure path to earthly and, especially, eternal
happiness. Outside of this path, happiness is
only apparent, though definitely appealing, to a
couple undergoing difficult moments. Sooner or
later, those who opt for these false and apparent
solutions will realize that that their nagging
sense of guilt and disquiet is a result of having
turned their backs on God's clear command:
*What therefore God has joined together, let no man
put asunder.*[31] Do away with that idea that to
break the matrimonial bond will solve all your
problems.
- The well-being of society. The "easy way out"
demeans the value and dignity of an institution
that builds a society. Experience shows that the
agglomeration of unions contracted after a divorce—
which are frequent and inevitable—gravely
damage the social fiber.

Be calm

Do not make hasty decisions while in the middle
of a crisis situation. Remember that passions obscure the
mind. Let the storm pass.

[31] Mt 19:6.

Do not lose hope

A couple may be tempted to think that there will never be peace in the house as long as they continue living together. Or that things will get worse or, in digging up old grudges, that everything had been a farce. This happens to all married couples. They look at the past in the light of their present problems. Everything has a solution if both sincerely work at a reconciliation, with the help of their loved ones. Moreover, God's grace will never fail for those who received the sacrament of Matrimony.

Dialogue

Talking it over is the best remedy if this is done with full sincerity, understanding, patience, and openness to what the other is saying. Pay careful attention, listen, understand and welcome your partner's reasons, attitudes, yearnings, and hurt feelings. To achieve this, take note of the list of factors that can short-circuit communication between spouses. Examine the causes of conflict and see what you can do to avoid them.

Identify points that you can agree on

These are many if you fight the temptation to magnify your differences. To love is to accept one another, including all of his or her shortcomings. Never try to squeeze the other into your own mould.

Avoid blaming each other

Stop finding out who is at fault. Surely, to a good measure both are to blame. Focus instead on fixing the problem.

Be ready to acknowledge and to make up for mistakes

This is what we have called the virtue of humility.

Forgive

Do not be surprised that two people who have lived together for long would consciously or unconsciously hurt one another in word or deed. If we do not forgive from the bottom of our hearts, grudges will pile up and become increasingly difficult to erase in time. Despite this, those who seek to reconcile must make the effort to clean the heart of any grudges, complaints or suspicions. One can never live together in peace as long as past hurts keep on surfacing. Let us ardently ask the Lord *to forgive us our sins as we forgive those who sin against us.*

Never stop struggling

Sincere, persevering and self-sacrificing struggle can solve many crises. Remember that valuable things cost a lot. The couple must take all the time and means needed to reconcile before resorting to a separation.

Seek advice from a family friend, counselor or priest

It is tough playing both judge and aggrieved party. Subjective views distort a case. Passions blur the mind and make it hard to accept and forgive the mistakes of others and to acknowledge one's own. For this and more reasons one ought to bring in a third party to help solve the problem. This person must be trustworthy and have a sound understanding of the nature and goals of marriage and the family.

Trust in God

We run to God for everything—in good times, in the midst of financial problems or other difficulties. What more reason to go to Him now that the happiness and stability of one's family are at stake. We must pray and to ask others to pray for us so that we may be enlightened and humble enough to see things as they are, in all truth and clarity. We also must ask for the strength to deal with the difficulties.

In a crisis situation, the spouses must try to strengthen their spiritual life by frequenting the sacraments, seeking spiritual guidance and reading good books that will aid them in their present situation. It is also important to reflect on the supernatural significance of marriage as a divine vocation and a great sacrament. The couple must have confidence in the power of the sacramental grace that they received when they got married. They continue to receive it every day, not just to sustain their marriage, but also to improve it and to bring it to perfection.

Temporary separation

Generally, it is not advisable for couples to separate. The Church, in fact, discourages this.[32] However, temporary separation can remedy certain cases, such as adultery, the physical or spiritual danger of the spouse or the children, or the malicious and unjust abandonment of the home. Temporary separation may reduce the tension and avoid conflicts. It may help calm spirits so that the couple may realize their mistakes and want to go on living together in due time, that is once the cause of their separation ceases to be.

However, we must clarify that separation is not the same as the breaking or dissolution of the marital bond. It is rather a suspension of the spouses' rights and duties in all that has to do with common conjugal life, or their living together. Therefore, separated spouses cannot consider themselves free to establish a new relationship with another person, which is the sin of adultery, plain and simple.

[32] **Can. 1151** - Spouses have the obligation and the right to maintain their common conjugal life, unless a lawful reason excuses them. *Code of Canon Law Annotated*, Wilson & Lafleur Limitée, Montreal, 1993.

4

Fecund Love

The best way to understand anything is to find out what it was made for. When we are dealing with institutions directly established by God and which, therefore, expressly manifest his will, it is absolutely necessary to uphold the purpose given them by their Divine Author; otherwise, we shall not be able to understand their nature and their different properties. This is true whether such an institution belongs to the supernatural order—like the Catholic Church—, or to the natural order—like the institution of marriage. God gave Matrimony specific ends which pertain to the natural order, and therefore, apply to Catholic marriages—which is a sacrament—and to any other genuine marriage. This is why all matrimonial laws must uphold these ends as God-given and recognize that their acceptance lies beyond the scope of matters left to the free discussion of men.[1]

[1] Cf. J.A. Garcia Prieto and J. L. Pastor, *Marriage and Divorce*, Medellin, 1975.

The Magisterium of the Church, which authentically interprets natural law, expresses Catholic tradition by teaching that the primary end of marriage is the procreation and upbringing of children. This primary end is, by nature, inseparably linked with the mutual love that must constantly be fostered by the spouses.[2] Thus, in every marriage, love, sexuality, and procreation —the three constitutive elements of the conjugal union—are always interconnected and in harmony with one another. We shall now discuss how and why this is so.

Sexuality and Procreation

By observing the characteristic features of man and woman, we are led to ask: Why has nature made them so different and yet so complementary? Why do they have a specific anatomical structure? Why are they different physiologically as well as psychologically? Why do they complement each other despite all these differences? Why is there a strong attraction between

---

[2] "The God himself who said *it is not good for man to be alone* (Gen 2:18) and *who made man from the beginning male and female* (Mt 19:4), wishing to share with man a certain special participation in his own creative work, blessed male and female, saying, *Increase and multiply* (Gen 1:28). Hence, while not making the other purposes of marriage of less account, the true practice of conjugal love and the whole meaning of the family life which results from it, have this aim: that the couple be ready with stout hearts to cooperate with the love of the Creator and the Savior, who through them will enlarge and enrich his own family day by day." Vatican Council II, Pastoral Constitution *GS* 50.

the sexes? These questions may as well be left unanswered if we are to consider them under the light of human sexuality alone. For nature herself has linked sexuality with a purpose and tells us plainly that man was made male and female to bring into this world new beings of the same species.

Reason and faith tell us that the sexual act, along with the pleasure that goes with it, is ordained toward the begetting of children. If it were otherwise, then why should there be two sexes? The sexual drive serves to facilitate and ensure the preservation of the species. Whenever a man and a woman engage in the sexual act, they set in motion a series of biological and physiological processes that are naturally directed towards giving birth to new life.

To understand this more easily, we can look at how God provided man with a number of natural incentives to help him fulfill his duty of preserving his existence. Imagine, for instance, how difficult it would be to eat if God had not attached a special pleasure to taking food. There is pleasure in eating precisely because nature meant this enjoyment to be an incentive for man to nourish himself. For who would want to spend so much time in front of a table ingesting food if it were not for that irresistible appetite, called hunger, and for the satisfaction and pleasure derived from eating? Thus man fulfills the need to keep himself alive through eating. What other purposes would hunger and the delights of eating have if not to encourage man to nourish himself?

Similarly, we can imagine how sorely neglected the preservation of the species would be without the strong sexual drive which God implanted in man. If there were no pleasure in sex, if there were no joy in loving and in having children and watching them grow, then hardly anyone would undertake the difficult mission of being a parent. Bringing up a family and educating children entail so much sacrifice that nature herself, to make it attractive, provided man with incentives to use his power to procreate and so assure the continuance of the human species.

The ordination of sexuality to procreation is therefore something natural and logical. Human sexuality is a positive reality which no one has the right to despise; and God himself, the Author of nature, has wanted it that way. He solemnly expressed his will in this regard when he made man male and female, commanding them at the same time to *increase and multiply*. For this reason, to arouse and satisfy the sexual drive without regard for the responsibility it entails breaks the link between sexual activity and procreation and thus constitutes an abuse of human sexuality. This abuse is precisely what Christian morality calls a sin against chastity, the virtue that leads one not to scorn or disdain sexual enjoyment but to recognize its great worth and noble purpose as seen in the over-all plan of the Creator.

"Sex is not a shameful thing; it is a divine gift, ordained to life, to love, to fruitfulness. This is the context in which we must see the Christian doctrine on sex. Our faith does not ignore anything on this earth that is beautiful, noble, and authentically human. It simply teaches us that the rule of our life should not be the selfish pursuit of pleasure because only sacrifice and self-denial lead to true love. God already loves us;

and now he invites us to love him and others with the truthfulness and sincerity with which he loves."[3]

Christian teaching does not look at sex as something negative or degrading; neither does it merely tolerate sex as a necessary evil brought about by original sin for the sake of preserving the human species. On the other hand, it would be far removed from Christian doctrine to regard sex as a mere source of pleasure. In this case, a person seeks maximum sexual satisfaction as an end, even if it would mean resorting to contraceptive devices to avoid the responsibilities of parenthood, or to limiting one's self to one or two children since a bigger number would entail more sacrifice.

The first misconception about sex as a negative phenomenon springs from a dualist outlook in life whereby spiritual realities are considered good, while anything that has to do with the flesh is evil. This view is the result of forgetting that both soul and body are creatures of God and that God can never be the source or origin of evil. Should this misconception influence a person, it would be impossible for him to appreciate the nobility of sex as the means God chose to make man share in his creative work.

From the very start, Christian teachings have always approached the subject of human sexuality in an enlightened way. Likewise, Christianity always had to defend herself against many misinterpretations. These errors first appeared under the form of Persian dualism, and were later on revived by Neoplatonism, Gnosticism, and Manicheanism. According to these philosophies, the differences between the sexes are

[3] *Christ is Passing By* no. 24.

defects in the human form which were not foreseen in the original design of creation; later on, however, either because of the influence of an evil principle or as a punishment for man's fall, they became part of human nature.[4] Subtle traces of this misconception live on in many areas of contemporary Western thought.

Christian doctrine, on the other hand, upholds that the differences between man and woman are part of the Creator's wise and loving plan. *Then God said, 'Let us make man in our image, after our likeness...' So God created man in his own image, in the image of God he created him; male and female he created them.*[5] St Paul himself openly condemned the stand of the Gnostics in his letter to Timothy. *Now the Spirit expressly says that in later times some will depart from the faith by giving heed to deceitful spirits and doctrines of demons, through the pretensions of liars whose consciences are seared, who forbid marriage and enjoin abstinence from foods which God created to be received with thanksgiving by those who believe and know the truth. For everything created by God is good...*[6]

The second misconception sees sex as a mere instrument of pleasure. This is a product of a materialistic and selfish outlook whereby the gratification of the sensible appetites is considered the primary objective. Consequently, the meaning of human sexuality is distorted by attributing to it an inadequate end. It becomes a means to obtain pleasure and therefore allows the use of anything and everything possible to maximize its enjoyment, even if these clearly

[4] Cf. Card. Joseph Hoffner, *Marriage and Family*, Madrid, pp. 14-16.

[5] Gen 1: 26, 27.

[6] 1 Tim 4:1-4.

run counter to nature. One therefore ends up falling into the aberrations that St Paul severely reproved centuries ago and which continue to exist today in a world that boasts of great social and technological achievements.[7] And when man abandons God in the pursuit of unbridled pleasure, he then commits the ultimate act of self-worship. We recall the strong and clear words of the Archangel Raphael as he persuaded young Tobias to marry Sarah: *Heed me well… and thou shalt hear why the fiend has power to hurt some and not others. The fiend has power over such as go about their marrying with all thought of God shut out of their hearts and minds, wholly intent on their lust, as if they were horse or mule, brutes without reason.*[8]

In an age when much progress has been made to promote and uphold human dignity, so many people paradoxically defend ideas that degrade men and women. With utter disregard for human freedom, various sectors of the mass media are being used to disseminate such views. In one way or another, the press, radio, television, film, literature, and advertising echo these

[7] *Therefore God gave them up in the lusts of their hearts to impurity, to the dishonoring of their bodies among themselves, because they exchanged the truth about God for a lie and worshiped and served the creature rather than the Creator, who is blessed forever! Amen. For this reason God gave them up to dishonorable passions. Their women exchanged natural relations for unnatural, and the men likewise gave up natural relations with women and were consumed with passion for one another, men committing shameless acts with men and receiving in their own persons the due penalty for their error. And since they did not see fit to acknowledge God, God gave them up to a base mind and to improper conduct.* Rom 1:24-28.

[8] Tob 6:16-17.

ideas and, through them, brutally suppress—often, successfully—any contrary idea. In the face of this materialistic and selfish attitude, the Christian continues to affirm that sex is naturally and supernaturally directed towards an end that goes beyond the sensual or animal in man. "Human love—pure, sincere and joyful—cannot subsist in marriage without the virtue of chastity, which leads couples to respect the mystery of sex and ordain it to faithfulness and personal dedication."[9]

Procreation and the mutual good of the spouses are the *raison d'etre* of human sexuality. If the sexual act were not necessary to engender new life, then obviously sex would have no meaning. God would not have created man male and female. It is therefore pointless to use sex for other purposes. However, this does not mean that sexual intercourse becomes illicit or meaningless if procreation is temporarily or even permanently rendered impossible due to biological reasons, such as sterility, menopause, or infertile periods. In such cases, the sexual act retains its importance and value as a means for the spouses to express their love for each other. It is also wrong to think that, given the said situations, it would be illicit to engage in the sexual act unless the couple has that conscious desire to have children. One cannot be obliged to desire an effect that is physiologically impossible. Thus the sexual act, despite the couple's inability to have children, is not only licit but also holy and sacred as long as it is done observing the reasonable norms of sexual morality in marriage.

[9] *Christ is Passing By* no. 25.

Love and Procreation

Conjugal love, like human sexuality, is naturally ordained to procreation. Love in this context is not mere friendship but a strong attraction between one man and one woman that moves them to desire a spiritual and physical union that will last a lifetime. This attraction naturally stems from the desire to perpetuate the species which God placed in man to ensure the conservation of the human species. In man, this desire is regulated by the intelligence and the will, in contrast with that of brute animals, which is governed by instinct.

A man and a woman attract and desire each other and fall in love because they are inclined by nature to seek not only personal fulfillment in mutual love but also the begetting and conservation of other rational beings. This kind of love never drains a person's capacity to love in different ways, say as a parent, son, friend, or as a creature adoring his Creator. This love is properly called "conjugal" for the specific properties and characteristics that we have mentioned above.

Needless to say, the value of conjugal love is not limited to its procreative function, since every kind of genuine love, taken in itself, has great worth. A couple does not fall in love just because they want to have children but because they feel a strong attraction to give all of themselves to each other. Even so, granting the intrinsic value of such a love, it remains true that conjugal love exists because of the natural need to preserve the species. If the human race were to be preserved through means other than sexual reproduction, then matrimonial love would not have been part of God's design on creation. The Second Vatican Council clearly affirmed this: "...the true practice of conjugal love, and the whole meaning of family life which results from it, have this aim: that the couple be ready with stout heart to cooperate with the love of the Creator and the Savior, who through them will enlarge and enrich his own family day by day."[10] Conjugal love therefore acquires its full meaning if it is ordained towards the begetting of new lives. This is true even if the spouses know that their intimate union cannot lead to conception because of physiological reasons. Even in this case, the love of the spouses would still be naturally linked with paternal love since children are the natural fruit of such self-giving.[11]

Every kind of love always begets something new, for love is like a vital force that gives rise to a new being. Take, for instance, the developments in the different fields of knowledge. These are products of the effort of people who have dedicated themselves to the task, not for its sake alone but, above all, for what they have foreseen as the objectives and gains of their endeavor. Progress in these fields is the fruit of the tenacious and diligent effort of such people. On the other hand, when science or politics is loved and pursued for its own sake, without considering the benefits it may bring to others, the end-product is usually obtained with a closed and narrow-minded outlook.

[10] Vatican Council II, Pastoral Const. *Gaudium et spes*, no. 50.

[11] "Conjugal love reveals its true nature and nobility when it is considered in its supreme origin, God, who is Love (cf. 1 Jn 4:8), *the Father, from whom every family in heaven and on earth is named* (Eph 3:15). Paul VI, *HV* 8.

"Love is essentially creative. Love of nature inspires the artist to create...And the mutual love of the spouses leads them to perpetuate themselves in their children. A person who has no desire to perpetuate his own likeness and that of his spouse in a fascinating variety of children has no genuine love either. Such a person is selfish, remains enclosed within himself, and is incapable of communicating with others. It is not a community of love that he forms with his spouse but a common life of selfishness."[12]

Spouses who plug up the wellsprings of life that God has given them end up regarding each other as unhappy accomplices in sin rather than loving partners in marriage. Again, this does not mean that spouses who are temporarily or definitely incapable of having children cannot truly love each other. They cultivate this love as something of great value in itself and, through it, work at edifying and ennobling each other.

Love and Sexuality

We have already explained in various ways the close bond between conjugal love and sexuality. Love should involve both the spiritual and the physical sides of man, for to exclude either of the two would destroy the very nature of love. If conjugal love were reduced to the mere enjoyment of sex, the spiritual side of man—his most important dimension—would be forgotten. He would in no way be different from brute

[12] Jean de Fabreges, *Christian Marriage*, Andorra, 1962, 102-103.

animals in this respect. On the other hand, to limit conjugal love to purely spiritual dealings, denying the spouses the right to the union of their bodies, is to dehumanize the marital relationship. It would exclude from conjugal love an essential element of the human person, a being who not only "inhabits" matter but is corporal by nature. Either of these two extreme attitudes, therefore, would seriously damage the love that leads to the perfection of husband and wife.

It follows that human sexuality finds its proper place only within the framework of conjugal love, understood as an embracing of the totality of the human person. The sexual relationship by itself cannot be meaningful when it is disconnected from its radical end. "Love that is exclusively carnal and directed only to the pursuit of sheer pleasure is in no way a total love. If the union between husband and wife is to be truly human and complete, spouses must give themselves to it entirely, both in body and in soul."[13] The union of two human beings in marriage will therefore reach perfection only if it involves a communication of the deepest aspects of their personalities. This loving interpersonal encounter is essentially a fusion of two lives, both in body and in soul, which is essentially what marriage is. If their mutual encounter were limited only to sex, then their encounter would necessarily be superficial, lacking in depth, wealth and content.[14] Experts have identified four disastrous consequences of breaking away from the natural integrity of conjugal love.

[13] Jacques Leclerq, *Christian Marriage*, Ediciones Rialp, 15th ed., 213.

[14] J. de Fabreges, *op. cit.*, 101.

First of all, it damages the loving union which should lead to the spouses' mutual enrichment. According to Sylvester Birngruber, "In authentic love, the pursuit of spiritual values is what is most important and must always be given priority. The physical encounter of two people constitutes, as it were, the culmination of the spiritual aspirations that they share. It is the visible symbol, expressed through their bodies, of the union of their souls ... If the demands of nature are to be respected, the union of bodies never takes place at the beginning, but at the end of a chain of events. Sexual intercourse without spiritual love that has reached a certain degree of maturity is an irresponsible act that does much harm instead of good."[15]

Second, deep-seated frustration and emptiness. Jean de Fabreges explains: "Whoever attempts to separate the carnal from the spiritual ends up losing both. For on one hand, he would deprive himself of the true joys that the proper use of the body can give; and on the other hand, he would never know the meaning of genuine spiritual fulfillment since this can only be achieved in an atmosphere of love...The flesh, therefore, ends up becoming a prison for such a person. Isolated from the rest of men by the thick walls of selfishness, his lot is one of constant loneliness. If he loves, he reaches out to no one but himself and even then he reaches only the external core of his personality. This is because the flesh wanted for its own sake is a dead-end route, a prison chamber, a veritable hell on earth."[16]

[15] Sylvester Birngruber, *Lay Morality*, Madrid, 1957, p. 319.
[16] J. de Fabreges, *op. cit.*, 102-103.

Third, the genuine intimacy between husband and wife would be lost and their encounter, instead of a loving relationship, would be a vile and degrading affair. "To become physically intimate with another person without any view to becoming spiritually intimate is a mark of vulgarity. It is to intimately associate one's self with someone only casually known. It makes love utterly cheap and worthy to be reckoned as most degrading."[17] Unfortunately, this is what happens in a home where the relationship between husband and wife is inspired not by love but by selfishness. The marriage bed, which should be holy because it is a reality that ought to be sanctified and which should sanctify, becomes no better than a harlot's couch.

Lastly, the couple's entire outlook would be inevitably impoverished. They easily end up living as though sexual enjoyment were the be-all-and-end-all in life. Love and marriage would have no other meaning outside of instinctive gratification. They would be incapable of a loving interpersonal relationship since they choose to give free rein to whims and passions instead of living up to the demands of sacrifice and generosity in marriage. Unhappy themselves, they are unable to secure happiness for others.

Spouses in this condition logically end up losing their appreciation for the higher values specific to man, which are those of the spirit. They become indifferent to the needs of their soul. Spiritual impoverishment makes their lives utterly empty and aimless. Naturally, the supernatural values are the first to languish as

[17] J. Leclerq, *op. cit.*, 213.

these are inevitably distasteful and bothersome to people given to loose living. One gradually loses one's faith and sense of religion and ends up completely turning his back to God.[18]

Marriage: Love, Sexuality and Procreation

The three factors which we have tackled separately are naturally and wonderfully intertwined in matrimony. In reality, we can compress them in two—love and procreation— because sexuality cannot be taken independently from the entire context of marriage. And if we go deeper, love and procreation can be reduced to just one element, which is love. For love is a creative and fecund force whose natural outcome is the begetting of children.

[18] Cf. S. Birngruber, *op. cit.*, 332-333.

5

Responsible Parenthood

The term has been an immensely popular buzzword in the past century even as it continues to be understood in many different ways. This is why it is timely to consider this Christian virtue in its various aspects.

Marriage is a state in life and a solid institution within which a man and a woman commit themselves to live together as man and wife for their entire life. The infinite consequences of this relationship affect the spouses—as individual persons and as a couple—, as well as their children and any one who comes in touch with them by virtue of their marriage. Husband and wife are therefore responsible for their love and for everything else that arises from their mutual self giving. There are responsibilities that must be fulfilled out of justice, while there are those that must be realized because one will have to account for them.

To get married is a free act, and so the human person is always responsible for one's love and for the outcome of that love. Thus bringing forth new lives assumes a dimension deeper than that of mere biological reproduction, which is an act proper to lesser beings. To give birth to a person is not just about giving one a physical body: It is to give rise to a complete human existence. "Paternity and maternity in the world of persons are certainly not limited to the biological function of transmitting life. Their significance is much deeper, and must be so in as much as the transmitter of life, father or mother, is a person. Paternity and maternity in the world of persons are the mark of a certain spiritual perfection, the capacity for "procreation" in the spiritual sense, the forming of souls. So that spiritual paternity and maternity have a much wider significance than physical parenthood. A father and mother who have given their children life in the merely biological sense must then supplement physical parenthood by spiritual parenthood, taking whatever pains necessary for their education."[1]

The Notion of Responsibility

What does it mean to be responsible? A responsible person is one capable of freely assuming the consequences of whatever he does or does not do. He is capable of dealing with every situation, guided by the right moral principles. By acting in this manner, he is prepared to render an account of his behavior to God, to his own conscience, and to all those he is responsible for, in one way or another. A person is

[1] Karol Wojtyla, *Love and Responsibility*, Ignatius Press, San Francisco, 1993, 260.

responsible for his actions in the first place to God, because he is subject to God in everything, and is therefore answerable to him for everything that he thinks, says and does. One lives this responsibility by acting in accordance with one's conscience, the inner voice that judges the goodness or evil of one's acts on the basis of an objective moral law. Moreover, because man is a social being, he must also answer for all the actions or omissions that affect his family and his community.

Obviously, a mature person is responsible person. Responsibility is a fruit of freedom and maturity. A mature person knows and practices the virtues that can mold his personality. And only a virtuous person can truly and freely account for his conduct. For example, children and the mentally impaired, to the extent that they lack reason, are not fully responsible for what they say or do. The same holds for people who are coerced into committing certain acts, or who do things out of fear, surprise or sheer exhaustion. Cowards can never be responsible people; neither can the nervous and the high-strung or the impulsive; much less those who are habitually indiscreet, self-centered, lazy, or comfort-seeking. A mature person, by contrast, is prudent in speech, judicious in his decisions, and careful but not indecisive in fulfilling his duties.

A mature person accepts himself as he is. He recognizes his limitations, patiently bears their consequences, and yet strives to overcome them. He makes up his mind with complete freedom and does not allow himself to be pressured into doing things. He is not like a little boy who vacillates between two alternatives because he is not sure of what he wants or is hesitant to employ the means to attain his objective. Self-assuredness, however, has nothing to do with pride. One, in fact, will discover that such a person is humble, simple, sincere, and straightforward. Lying, on the other hand is the mark of a weak person. A mature and responsible person keeps his word and is faithful to his duties. He never shirks a task but rather sees it as an opportunity to serve others. He is ready to face the consequences of loving, not like a capricious adolescent who easily gets swayed by passion and the delights of the senses.

All these qualities bestow one with inner fulfillment characterized by resoluteness and equanimity of spirit, which, for a Christian is derived from "personal reflection, which endeavors in all humility to grasp the will of God in both the unimportant and the important events of his life."[2]

A responsible person is not dazzled by brilliant but fly-by-night ideas or slogans that effectively manipulate weak minds. Emotionally, he lives up to his commitments of fidelity and knows how to control the affections of the heart. He is disciplined and therefore acts coherently and reasonably; he does not disconcert people with inconstant, fickle, disloyal or hypocritical behavior.

It is not easy to be responsible especially when it comes to siring and educating children. To be a parent is to live up to certain human and supernatural commitments which have deep and definite repercussions on the upbringing of children—even on those who are yet to be born.

---

[2] *Conversations...* no. 116.

Adequate Preparation

One is not born mature and responsible. It takes time and constant effort to be so. This is why St Paul exhorts the Christians in Ephesus *to attain to the unity of the faith and of the knowledge of the Son of God, to mature manhood, to the measure of the stature of the fullness of Christ, so that we may no longer be children, tossed to and from and carried about with every wind of doctrine, by the cunning of men, by their craftiness in deceitful wiles.*[3] Christian living calls for balanced judgment and sound discernment, interior stability and full accountability for one's acts. But this cannot be achieved through mere desire; one must cultivate it.

Irrational animals have no need to go beyond mere physiological parenting which for them is instinctive and mechanical. The rational nature of man, on the other hand, leads him to inquire into why things are so and how he can achieve his goals. The role of human parents is a lifetime one and extends to the life hereafter. Thus:

"In particular, responsible fatherhood and motherhood directly concern the moment in which a man and a woman, uniting themselves "in one flesh," can become parents. This is a moment of special value both for their interpersonal relationship and for their service to life: they can become parents—father and mother—by communicating life to a new human being... They then experience a moment of special responsibility, which is also the result of the procreative potential linked to the conjugal act. At that moment, the spouses can become father and mother, initiating the process of

[3] Eph 4:13-14.

begetting a new human life, that will then develop in the woman's womb. If the wife is the first to realize that she has become a mother, the husband, to whom she has been united in "one flesh," then learns this when she tells him that he has become a father. Both are responsible for their potential and, later, actual fatherhood and motherhood. The husband cannot fail to acknowledge and accept the result of a decision which has also been his own. He cannot hide behind expressions such as 'I don't know,' 'I didn't want it,' or 'You're the one who wanted it.' In every case, conjugal union involves the responsibility of the man and of the woman, a potential responsibility which becomes actual when the circumstances dictate. This is true especially for the man. Although he, too, is involved in the beginning of the generative process, he is left biologically distant from it; it is within the woman that the process develops. How can the man fail to assume responsibility? The man and the woman must assume together, before themselves and before others, the responsibility for the new life which they have brought into existence."[4]

Since human paternity is not a mere biological task but a difficult, lifelong mission, one needs to be adequately prepared for it. A person who wants to become an engineer spends years of effort and sacrifice to obtain the qualifications. Another who wants to become a doctor must devote even double the time studying because so many lives will depend on him. An aspiring priest should devote much time to prayer, study and apostolic work so that he can effectively fulfill his mission of leading souls to Heaven. This

[4] John Paul II, *Letter to Families* no. 12.

proves that all formation, difficult as it may be, is important because no one can do a job responsibly without the required knowledge and skills.

To be a responsible parent, one must first have the humble disposition to be educated and so be sufficiently prepared to live up to the demands of forming a family. It is unfortunate to see so many young people casually jump into forming a home and having children when they sorely lack the human and spiritual qualifications for the job. In short, they approach the serious task of marriage and parenthood with frivolity. If there were only special degree courses in parenthood, then we can also qualify parents as mediocre and ill-fitted for the job in the same way we would judge a negligent engineer, an incompetent doctor, or a superficial priest. A responsible parent works on impeccable standards and is thoroughly aware of the commitments involved in raising a family. A person who intends to get married must therefore prepare one's self for future responsibilities by reading good books on the topic. One ought to seek the advice of prudent persons and open one's mind and heart to God's voice and commandments. If such preparation was neglected before one got married, then it is all the more urgent— and never too late—to work on it now.

The Responsibility to have Children

The first aspect of responsible parenthood that we ought to tackle is knowledge and respect for the biological process. Married couples must know the natural laws that govern human sexuality and hold them in great esteem. Secondly, as regards the tendencies of instinct or passion, responsible parenthood means developing self-mastery so as to subject the said tendencies to reason and not be led by the impulses of a disordered concupiscence.

Responsible parenthood also leads spouses to deliberate on the number of children they can have, using a correct and well-formed conscience as the basis of their decisions. They must consider their physical, economic, psychological, and social circumstances and decide whether, through a deliberate and generous decision, they can raise a numerous family. If not, because of serious motives and with due respect for the moral law, they temporarily or even indefinitely avoid a new birth. Spouses must remember that they will render an account to God for every child they choose to have or not to have. Parents who thoughtlessly beget as many children as the wife is physically capable of having are as irresponsible as those who, for no serious reason, refuse to collaborate with God in raising up new lives.[5]

[5] Vatican Council II explains: "Parents should regard as their proper mission the task of transmitting human life and educating those to whom it has been transmitted. They should realize that they are thereby cooperators with the love of God the Creator and are, so to speak, the interpreters of that love. Thus, they will fulfill their task with human and Christian responsibility and, with docile reverence towards God, will make decisions by common counsel and effort. Let them thoughtfully take into account both their own welfare and that of their children, those already born, and those which the future may bring. For this accounting, they need to reckon with both the material and the spiritual conditions of the times as well as of their state in life. Finally, they should consult the interests of the family group, of temporal society, and of the Church herself." Pastoral Constitution GS 50.

As regards deciding on the number of children they should have, the spouses must understand and observe the dictates of a well-formed conscience (as the name implies, conscience is the "science," that is, "knowledge" of the moral law). This presupposes that husband and wife know the objective moral norms involved and have considered all the consequences of their decision. They must bear in mind that every one of their actions will be reckoned as deserving of reward or punishment because these are the result of a free and deliberate choice.

Spouses must consider their conscience as the voice of God. For Christians, it is also the voice of Christ and his Church. This means that all our conscious acts must be inspired by a mind enlightened by serious reflection, where the will of God and the teaching of Christ's representatives on Earth must always be followed. Hence, the Second Vatican Council, after affirming that the spouses, and no one else, should ultimately decide on the number of children they should have, they must also be aware that they cannot proceed arbitrarily. Their conscience must always dutifully conform to the divine law and submit to the Church, whose teaching office authentically interprets the law in the light of the Gospel.

Responsible parenthood, then, is not merely a question of having as many children as the wife is physically capable of bearing; neither is it a matter of using artificial means to avoid conception. The decision to have a child must be made in God's presence, adhering to the moral law. The transmission of life is a mission and certainly a divine task because God is directly involved in it.

The Supernatural Demands
of Responsible Parenthood

While one must "honor one's father and mother," the Fourth Commandment also works the other way: Parents, too, must *honor their children*. In the context of the ten Commandments, to "honor" means to serve, acknowledge, attend to, take care of, and give one's self to someone. These are all excellent ways of loving.

"If the Fourth Commandment demands that honor should be shown to our father and mother, it also makes this demand out of concern for the good of the family. Precisely for this reason, however, it makes demands on the parents themselves. You parents, the divine precept seems to say, should act in such a way that your life will merit the honor (and the love) of your children! Do not let the divine command that you be honored fall into a moral vacuum! Ultimately then we are speaking of *mutual honor*. The commandment "honor your father and your mother" indirectly tells parents: Honor your sons and your daughters. They deserve this because they are alive, because they are who they are, and this is true from the first moment of their conception."[6]

As in many other areas of human life, responsible parenthood makes supernatural demands on Christian fathers and mothers because God's designs concerning marriage go beyond purely natural ends. One's conscience must be attuned to God's way of thinking and wanting things; in other words, his specific plans for each married couple. Human love is authentic only to the measure that it is inspired by and seeks the love

[6] John Paul II, *Letter to Families*, 1994, no. 15.

of God. In the same way, mutual self-giving in marriage attains its full meaning if the supernatural purpose of procreation is respected. For a Christian, to beget a child entails assuming responsibility for its eternal destiny, and responsible parenthood means carrying out this duty faithfully. Human parenthood means much more than just siring offspring—irrational animals do as much. It also means educating them, preparing them for life, and guiding their steps towards eternal salvation. What good would parents have accomplished in feeding, clothing and pampering their children if they neglect their principal duty of leading them to happiness on earth and to the indescribable joys of the life hereafter? There is no point in lavishing so much care on one's children here on earth, only to leave them afterwards to eternal damnation because they were not taught how to love and worship God and to honor their neighbor. *For what will it profit a man, if he gains the whole world and forfeits his life?*[7]

Educating one's children is never improvised. For this, one must be equipped with human fortitude and supernatural faith and charity. For a Christian only in name, this will then be an enormously daunting task. Parents must strive to be holy if they want to teach their children to love God. *Be perfect as your Father in heaven is perfect.*[8] Without the effort to practice the virtues, the call to the fullness of Christian life may just as well be a beautiful but unattainable goal.

It is not surprising then to see many lukewarm Christians—Christians hardly imbued with the Gospel spirit—reacting negatively when the Church makes a

[7] Mt 16: 26.
[8] Cf. Mt 5:48.

pronouncement that clearly marks the route to follow in order to reach salvation. This is what is happening with the Church's stand on birth control. Many feel themselves unable to follow it. The Cross, however, will always remain the true sign of the Christian even if it scares away those who wish to hear nothing of struggle, sacrifice and generosity with God. The perennial teaching of the Church on this matter will always appear difficult and impractical to many because all great realities demand serious effort on the part of the person, the family, and society itself. Moreover, this teaching would be hard to practice without God's help, since it is He who sustains and strengthens the good will of men.

For a Christian conscience, a problem will never have a purely human solution. Partial answers will never suffice for situations that involve one's entire life. A real Christian always lives according to one's Faith and generously accepts all the sacrifices that this entails. Devotions of piety, no matter how many or how sincerely one prays them, are of no help if these are divorced from other important aspects of one's life. The responsibilities of a Christian father or mother call for serious personal formation. An ignorant person cannot be responsible for what he does; neither can one simply pick out the commandments that he would like to follow. One can live all aspects of the Catholic Church's teaching only if he is determined and if he has the interior strength to obey all of God's commandments everywhere and at any time.

Evidently, it takes effort to live up to the demands of the Faith because it involves an encounter with the Cross of Christ. For a Christian, the Cross should never be an empty symbol. As St Paul put it, the Cross is foolishness to some and a scandal to others but for Christians, it is *the power and the wisdom of God.*[9] To understand the Cross, one needs to pray and to receive the sacraments; and of particular import is the frequent reception of sacramental Confession and the Holy Eucharist. This is the path of a Christian who wishes to be faithful to his vocation as parent and spouse and as a child of God and heir to his glory. Only by these means can a Christian find strength to use his generative powers responsibly and thus achieve conjugal harmony in the physical, affective, and spiritual dimensions of married love. One's marriage will then become a true act of mutual self-giving, in contrast with the merely legal contracts entered into by couples who want nothing of sacrifice and generosity. Conjugal love thus acquires a fullness and an authenticity that transcends instinct or passion: It opens itself to fulfilling the divine will. A love that therefore becomes more perfect as it engenders in the spouses the yearning to beget life which moves them to love their children even before they come into existence.

Feeling Totally Responsible for One's Children

As we have seen, parenthood is not a mere biological function. What father and mother have engendered out of love must also be cared for with love. Both spouses then assume full responsibility for their child's upbringing. Just as they freely and purposely helped

[9] Cf. 1 Cor 1:23-25.

to form this new life together, so, too, together they face the challenges that the fruit of their union brings. In a word, father and mother are called to respond to their child's needs, not only at the start but all throughout its earthly life.

"A child is not something owed to one, but is a gift. The 'supreme gift of marriage' is a human person. A child may not be considered a piece of property, an idea to which an alleged 'right to a child' would lead. In this area, only the child possesses genuine rights: the right 'to be the fruit of the specific act of conjugal love of his parents, 'and the right to be respected as a person from the moment of his conception."[10]

Responsible as they have been for the child's conception, the parents must likewise be responsible for its present and its future. The formation and affection, the discipline, and the experiences of care and rigor all leave a deep and lasting impression on the character of this new human being. Although we are born free and free we should always be, we must never forget that human nature is weak on account of the consequences of original sin. Children need help and guidance along their path towards maturity. And parents who faithfully fulfill this duty will experience the joy and the gratitude of the children whom they have educated in virtue.

The father and the mother are equally responsible for the formation of their children. They cannot shirk this grave moral obligation. Fathers, in particular, should resist the temptation of leaving the task to the mother on the comfortable excuse that they have

---

[10] *CCC* Word & Life Publications, Manila, 1994, no. 2378.

absorbing professional commitments. Such an attitude is not only one of seeking an easy way out; it is also ineffective, pedagogically speaking. A child at whatever age needs the active and constant presence of both parents. For one, he sometimes needs to discuss questions that are best brought up with the father alone or with the mother alone. He also needs both a masculine and a feminine touch to acquire a balanced personality. The strict hierarchy of values of one parent goes hand in hand with the ability of the other to handle unexpected situations. The child will benefit from the father's sober and logical approach to problems, as well as from the mother's sensitive and compassionate nature. In one parent, the child will have a stern guardian; in the other, a lively and cheerful companion.

By the very fact that they are different, both parents contribute to helping the child acquire a mature personality. Although the father would spend less time at home, he nevertheless should spend his after-work hours and, of course, the weekends, with his family. He must remember that a father or a mother's best and most important business is to be with the children. It would therefore be a mistake to pass the burden of the children's formation to the school, no matter how good the institution may be. The responsibility of bringing up the children always rests primarily on the parents, although it may be shared by an educational institution. A good school is, without doubt, the home's best complement, but never a substitute for it.[11]

[11] Cf. J. Abad and E. Fenoy, *Children*, Sinag-tala Publishers, Inc., Manila, 1995.

The Material Maintenance of the Home

Responsible parenthood also has its financial side. Without money, it is impossible to maintain the minimum standard of human dignity in the home. There are things that may be considered "extras" but which contribute to creating a cheerful, pleasant, and restful atmosphere. It would therefore be irresponsible for a father or a mother to neglect the material well-being of the home. Meals must be balanced and healthy and as generous as need be. The house must be clean, pleasant and cheerful, but not necessarily luxurious.

With a bit of good taste, a good house keeper can do amazing things with some backyard flowers and twigs. Parents should also see to it that everyone gets the necessary hours of sleep. Recreation must be varied, family games enjoyable and the air punctuated by good music. There are many things that can make a house a haven of peace and a training ground for virtues.

However, money alone achieves nothing even if it is indispensable to raising a family. To acquire money, one must work well and fulfill one's obligations responsibly. A husband usually holds a job as a means of livelihood. A wife, on the other hand, ordinarily takes care of the home even if, sometimes, personal or family circumstance may call for a different arrangement.

In different ways, husband and wife exert the effort to make daily life in the family a pleasant experience. Both must give untiring good example, be models of industriousness and reflect serene Christian optimism. Still, responsible parenthood does not end here because it covers a wide variety of areas. It is a matter of analyzing every aspect of family life and relationships to understand what it really is all about.

Motherhood and Professional Work

The work that a woman does in the home is, undoubtedly a genuine profession. Nevertheless, to pursue a career outside the home has become a woman's most irresistible dream. She is aware that her dignity makes her equal to man and that her many virtues and talents may be put to service of others, which is a positive and laudable aspiration. Women can contribute to social progress in the same way as men do.

Still, many—a sensible wife asks this question which is born, no doubt, of a Christian sense of duty: "Is my office job, which affords me some public recognition, much better than the effective but unassuming tasks that I carry out at home?" There is hardly a final, clear-cut answer to this, for both types of work are important and deserving of one's best efforts. However, one must never forget that the family is the basic unit of every human community. It is the nucleus around which the progress of society takes place, and the seedbed of the virtues and talents that prepare one for professional life.

"Even on the personal level, one cannot flatly affirm that a woman has to achieve her perfection only outside the home, as if time spent on her family were time stolen from the development of her personality. The home—whatever its characteristics, because a single woman should also have a home—is a particularly suitable place for the growth of her personality...What I have just said does not go against her participating in other aspects of social life, including politics. In these spheres, too, women can offer a valuable personal contribution without neglecting their special feminine qualities. They will do this to the extent in which they are humanly and professionally equipped."[12]

It is tempting to think—as happens often nowadays—that intellectual or manual work done outside the home is worth more than household work. A father and a mother who take good care of the home and the children make a priceless contribution to society, not only in the long-but in the short-run as well. A brilliant professional career that boasts economic, cultural or political achievements can never make up for the pain and guilt of having neglected one's children. Both activities are not necessarily incompatible; they can be pursued at the same time, provided one works in an orderly and efficient manner.

The children, for instance, can relieve their mother of some household concerns so that she may be able to spend some time for personal enrichment, such as getting involved in a social project or developing her artistic bent. Also, modern technology offers many time-saving devices that make household work easier and quicker to finish. With a bit of planning and the generous cooperation of all the members of the family, a wife can engage in work outside the home without neglecting her domestic responsibilities.

[12] *Conversations...* no. 87.

To summarize, a proper scale of values must inspire one's activities. Parents should realize that theirs is a God-given role and that it is the most important one that they can ever have. The noblest vocation is to participate in the creation of new life and to care for the proper education of one's offspring. Its bearing on society can never be overemphasized.

Sad to say, motherhood today is not as highly appreciated as the pursuit of a career outside the home. All efforts to restore its authentic value in the eyes of the world are therefore a welcome boon to women and society at large. It is certainly true that a woman's generous decision to bear new life in her womb entails much self-giving, courage and sacrifice.

Still, a mother's self-giving is a most pleasing offering to God, who, by entrusting an immortal soul to her care, gives clear proof of his confidence in her. Motherhood is a testimony to the enormous value of human life and the greatness of the mission every human being is called upon to carry out in the world.

In a visit to Ireland, Pope John Paul II exhorted married couples to hold their role as parents in high esteem. "Do not think that anything you do in life is more important than to be a good Christian father and mother. May Irish mothers, young women, and girls not listen to those who tell them that working in a secular job, succeeding in a secular profession, is more important than the vocation of giving life and caring for this life as a mother. The future of the Church, the future of humanity, depend in great part on parents and on the family life that they build in their homes."[13]

[13] Homily at the Mass in Limerick, October 1, 1979.

Our Christian principles must lead us to give every support to a woman who is expecting a child. She must not be left alone to face the doubts, difficulties and temptations that sometimes confront her during this critical period. She needs the support and the assurance that, in giving herself to this task, she is fulfilling one of the loftiest aspirations of the human heart. In his pastoral visits throughout the world, the Pope stresses the need to inspire courage in women who have not refused to assume the responsibility of motherhood. He reminds us to sustain their hope and to strengthen their conviction that, in opting to bring new life into this world, they choose to do good.

Motherhood is woman's vocation. It is the touchstone of her presence in the world. The present Pope once recalled a Polish song that praises woman as "the mother who understands everything and embraces each of us with her heart.""The world today is particularly 'hungry and thirsty' for that motherhood, which is woman's vocation 'physically' and 'spiritually,' as it is Mary's. Everything must be done in order that the dignity of this splendid vocation may not be broken in the inner life of the new generations; in order that the authority of the woman-mother may not be diminished in the family, social and public life, and in the whole of our civilization...in every field of life. This is a fundamental criterion. We must do everything in order that children, the family, and society may see in her that dignity that Christ saw, *Mater genetrix, spes nostra!*"[14]

[14] John Paul II, General audience, January 10, 1979.
[15] Cf. John Paul II, *Discourse to Workers*, Czestochowa, June 6, 1979.

It is therefore advisable to keep this reality in mind every time one starts to weigh professional concerns against family duties. Maternity deserves to be venerated and respected in society as a great end and a great mission in itself. The true respect for work brings with it due esteem for maternity, for on it depends the moral health of society.[15]

Woman and the Work in the Home

Work outside the home is not superior to or more "substantial" than household work. One cannot absolutely state that a woman fulfills herself more in the office than in the kitchen. It is also a fallacy to say that a woman makes more useful contributions to society when she pursues a career outside of the home. In fact, society for centuries has advanced without engineers, sociologists, economists or biologists; but things will never do without someone taking care of the household chores. Even the most sober and spiritual of men need a well-balanced diet, clean, well-ironed clothes and a home that is welcoming and clean.

Much of one's life develops and takes place in the home. There, one rests and replenishes lost energies and finds a chance to pursue one's interests and affections. It is in the home, moreover, where the children grow and acquire some of the most important features of their personality. Work in the home is indispensable for the smooth-sailing of human life and the family. It is the ideal environment for one to grow in bodily,

[16] *Conversations...* no. 87.

psychological and supernatural health. "The attention a woman gives to her family will always be her greatest dignity. In the care she takes of her husband and children or, to put it in more general terms, in her work of creating a warm and formative atmosphere around her, a woman fulfills the most indispensable part of her mission. And so it follows that she can achieve her personal perfection there."[16]

However man must also take interest in the things of the home. Dr. Philip Felig, a professor of medicine at the Yale University and chief of Endocrinology at the Yale-New Haven Hospital, shares how he got to better appreciate his wife's household work:

"Thrust temporarily into the role of homemaker during my wife's recent trip abroad, I learned to appreciate more directly the duties and satisfactions that housewives experience daily. First, work that I had taken for granted and had never done (meal preparation, kitchen clean-up, laundry), I quickly recognized would not be done unless I did it. Second, being a good parent required more than a cheery smile and willingness to help with the homework...

Initially, it all seemed like an endless succession of tedious detail. Yet I soon recognized that without me the family wouldn't run smoothly. It was I who provided a pleasant environment to which the children returned from school and to which I returned from my office. What I did as homemaker seemed far more meaningful to the family's existence than the income I was providing. Clearly, our daily happiness depended less on the size of my paycheck than on my wife's efficiency."[17]

[17] Philip Felig, "Confessions of a Surrogate 'Housewife'" *The New York Times*, February 11, 1978, 21.

Indeed, running a home requires a great amount of talent and virtue and, to those who devote their best energies to it, the job becomes an effective means for personal enrichment. Domestic work calls for continual and complete dedication and, therefore, is a daily exercise in asceticism that calls for patience, self-control, far-sightedness, creativity, flexibility, and courage in the face of the unexpected.[18] Furthermore, it fosters industriousness, constancy and a sense of responsibility, as well as develops virtues like serenity, cheerfulness, and good humor that help the family face the small difficulties of daily living with a smile. Family life then becomes a pleasant experience since everyone tries to be kind and to listen and be concerned about everybody else.[19]

Besides, domestic tasks are so hidden and unassuming that people usually ignore or take them for granted—which means a constant opportunity to grow in the virtue of humility. Everything is done for the love of God and the family. Dr. Felig continues:

"There were no grateful patients thanking me for keeping a clean kitchen. No applause from a large lecture hall after making sure the children left happily for school. No praise from a professional colleague for having kept up with the laundry. In short, my reward was entirely from within. I knew I was doing well because the children and I were happy and our needs were met but there was no outside recognition of that achievement. For a housewife, it is rare that her effectiveness is truly recognized...To spend a lifetime

[18] Cf. John Paul II Address in Rome, April 29, 1979.
[19] Cf. Francisca Rodriguez Quiroga, *El trabajo del hogar, una tarea esencial* (Unpublished).

of accomplishment with so few external rewards calls for a very strong personality..."[20]

Insofar as the welfare of society is concerned, it can truly be said that household work is of inestimable value since it is indispensable for the well-being of the family, which, in turn, is the foundation of all social life. From the confines of the home emerge future citizens who are prepared to do good to society. There, the citizens of today retire and get a recharge. Thus:

"The job of a woman in her house is a social contribution in itself; in fact, it can easily be classified as the most effective of all...Women are called to bring to the family, to society and to the Church characteristics which are their own and which they alone can give: their gentle warmth and untiring generosity, their love for detail, their quick-wittedness and intuition, their simple and deep piety, their constancy...A woman's femininity is genuine only if she is aware of the beauty of this contribution for which there is no substitute and if she incorporates it into her own life."[21]

It would then be very wrong for a woman to allow herself to be dazzled by the prospect of a career outside the home and as a consequence neglect the work which nature has especially equipped her for and in which she can achieve lasting fulfillment. This does not mean, of course, that a woman is not suited for any other job except household work or that she is necessarily inferior to man in other fields. A woman who is professionally prepared can definitely make significant contributions in her field of competence. What we wish to point out here is the danger of underrating specifically feminine qualities, the up-

[20] P. Felig, *op. cit.*

shot of which would be a misplaced zeal to imitate a man. In this case, the woman is the loser. She is neither superior nor inferior to man, but simply different from him. This difference does not suppress but fosters the human person's radical condition of equal dignity and the right to enjoy equal opportunities.

Woman has the triple role of spouse, mother, and heart of the home. They are hers by nature and cannot be transferred to anyone else. She enjoys the same dignity as man in society and together with him, she is called to work for the common good. However, says Pope Pius XII, "each of the two sexes must take the part which belongs to it according to its nature, its characteristics, its physical, intellectual, and moral habits...The woman has, generally speaking, more perspicacity and greater tact to help her understand and solve the delicate problems of domestic and family life, which is the foundation of all social life."[22]

Her role as a mother is of great importance. There is no substitute for her efforts to educate and to bring up the children. Many studies on child psychology confirm the positive effects of a mother's love on the psychological development of a child, especially as regards emotional maturity. All these facts should encourage a mother to spend her best energies in caring for the home and to avoid getting distracted by extra-domestic concerns (which, on the other hand, can always be made compatible with household work). The home is her most important responsibility and it should be a great joy for her to assume it.

[21] *Conversations...* no. 89.
[22] *Address to Women of Catholic Action*, October 21, 1945.

"When a mother, out of selfishness, neglects the home, she has to account for not imparting to her children the due example of a life of generous sacrifice and self-giving. Without a mother's care, the family hearth ceases to be a home. It becomes a simple boarding house whose residents only look after themselves. The family then loses the atmosphere of love that it needs in order to be a school of Christian virtues; instead, it becomes a training ground for selfish habits that later on bring a train of baneful effects on society. On the other hand, a mother's dedication to her domestic duties is in itself a valuable lesson to the children. It teaches them, not through words but by deeds that they can touch and feel, the genuine meaning of love and its expression in a life of disinterested service and sacrifice."[23]

Childless Couples

How about childless couples? Are they excluded from the duties and concerns of responsible parenting? How should a couple face the situation, without any fault on their part and in spite of their desire to have children, they remain childless? Naturally, the first step is to look for the possible cause; both husband and wife should seek opportune advice from a reliable physician and raise a humble prayer to God, Who is all good and powerful enough to bless them with children, if they ask for it perseveringly and confidently. But if in spite of the effort, no child would

[23] F. Rodriguez Quiroga, *op. cit.*

come, then the couple must learn to accept God's will and try to discover his hidden purposes. Perhaps He is "asking them to put the same effort and the same kind and gentle dedication into helping their neighbors as they would have put into raising their children, without the human joy that comes from having children. There is, then, no reason for feeling they are failures or for giving way to sadness."[24]

Since they are childless due to no fault of theirs, the couple must see in their condition a special call from Heaven, a different kind of blessing from God. They will not feel frustrated if they wholeheartedly strive to intensify the ardor of their mutual love. They must continue to sustain the desire to give themselves and to remain faithful to each other all throughout their lives.[25] Their lives therefore break away from the narrow confines of a self-centered existence: they have accepted the divine call to be spiritual parents by generously providing for the needs of charitable or apostolic undertakings.

If childless couples look around, they will discover many people in need, many who can profit from their attention, charity and affection. Their best energies, which otherwise would have been directed to their children, can thus be spent at the service of relatives, friends, and any one who suffers in body and spirit. In this new-found vocation, the couple will experience spiritual fruitfulness that will fill them with peace and happiness. Those who place no limits to their generosity and who devote themselves to working for the good of

[24] *Conversations...* no. 96.
[25] Cf. Gonzalo Lobo Mendez, *Person, Family, and Society*, Madrid, 1973, 184.

others are most certainly happy because those who give love will always receive double the joy of those who have benefited from their love.[26]

---

[26] "Fruitful married love expresses itself in serving life in many ways. Of these ways, begetting and educating children are the most immediate, specific and irreplaceable. In fact, every act of true love towards a human being bears witness to and perfects the spiritual fecundity of the family, since it is an act of obedience to the deep inner dynamism of love as self-giving to others.

For everyone this perspective is full of value and commitment, and it can be an inspiration in particular for couples who experience physical sterility.

Christian families, recognizing with faith all human beings as children of the same heavenly Father, will respond generously to the children of other families, giving them support and love not as outsiders but as members of the one family of God's children. Christian parents will thus be able to spread their love beyond the bonds of flesh and blood, nourishing the links that are rooted in the spirit and that develop through concrete service to the children of other families, who are often without even the barest necessities.

Christian families will be able to show greater readiness to adopt and foster children who have lost their parents or have been abandoned by them. Rediscovering the warmth of affection of a family, these children will be able to experience God's loving and provident fatherhood witnessed to by Christian parents, and they will thus be able to grow up with serenity and confidence in life. At the same time the whole family will be enriched with the spiritual values of a wider fraternity.

Family fecundity must have an unceasing 'creativity,' a marvelous fruit of the Spirit of God, who opens the eyes of the heart to discover the new needs and sufferings of our society and gives courage for accepting them and responding to them. A vast field of activity lies open to families: today, even more preoccupying than child abandonment is the phenomenon of

Adoption is another possibility, although this must be understood not just as a way of satisfying one's maternal yearning—legitimate in itself but which can be subtly tainted by selfishness—but as a wonderful way to offer an abandoned child a home. Today's prevalent lifestyle calls for childless couples to be concerned about every baby's future, since its own parents, for one reason or another, are incapable of giving it the ideal family atmosphere.

Adoptive parents can offer a child a family where it can be loved, educated and taught the meaning of generosity, thus assuring it the best possible earthly joy and a stable path to happiness in heaven. Adoption therefore is not just a matter of giving a child to parents who need one, but to offer it good parents and a good family environment.

Experience shows that the love of adoptive parents can be as real, if not greater than, the child's natural parents. Thus, an adopted child is no less its parents' own child, in the same way that Christians experience the reality of being adopted children of their heavenly Father.

---

social and cultural exclusion, which seriously affects the elderly, the sick, the disabled, drug addicts, ex-prisoners, etc.

This broadens enormously the horizons of the parenthood of Christian families: these and many other urgent needs of our time are a challenge to their spiritually fruitful love. With families and through them, the Lord Jesus continues to 'have compassion' on the multitudes." (FC 41).

The Role of the Household Help

Much of what we have said about the role of a housewife also applies to the hidden but valuable service rendered by the household help. Theirs is a mission that must be carried out professionally and, therefore, should never be despised. Here are some thoughts and positive insights of a woman who has spent practically her entire life employed as a domestic helper:

"Our type of work is neither humiliating nor insignificant. Colleagues of mine say that our work is degrading. They complain that it does not merit any recognition and that it is the least of all professions. They say that, given the chance, they would leave the job to work in a factory or a store—anything but household work. I have asked myself many times whether it would not be better to try to raise the standards of our profession so that those who come after us do not find themselves in the same predicament. We need to make our work a responsible and dignified profession that merits social recognition. But first, we ourselves must appreciate the value of what we do. It is no surprise then that people should look down on our work since we ourselves do not take pains to obtain for it due status in society."[27]

Domestic work is a well-defined professional vocation. It answers a definite need of the family and of society and consequently demands suitable preparation. So many things in the home depend on it: the

[27] María Teresa Sanchez, *Domestic Work: A Profession*, Sinagtala Booklet.

order and cleanliness, the meals, the wholesome and pleasant atmosphere. If a home should run smoothly, then a domestic helper must be industrious, charitable, discreet, loyal, self-sacrificing, patient, humble and orderly. She must also have one more virtue, which is called spirit of service. Far from lowering her dignity, the desire to serve elevates it. Service was a trademark feature of the Son of God, who came *not to be served, but to serve.*[28]

People nowadays may not like the idea of serving because the term has a humiliating connotation. However, when one gets to think about it, all jobs make for true and authentic service because they respond to a social need. Think of a street sweeper, a domestic helper, a university professor, or a judge. Perhaps it is only work done grudgingly or solely for selfish gain that may not qualify as a form of "service."

John Paul II had nothing but praise for the work of housekeepers when he addressed the 10th Assembly of the Professional Association of Family Collaborators of Italy (APICOLF):

"A necessary and indispensable work, a work of sacrifice which is not exciting. Work that does not win applause and sometimes not even recognition and gratitude; it is the humble, repeated, monotonous and therefore heroic work of an innumerable host of mothers and young women. Certainly, this work must be seen not as an implacable and inexorable imposition, a form of slavery, but as a free choice, responsible and willed, which completely fulfill a woman's needs and

---

[28] Mk 10:45.

personality. Domestic work, in fact, is an essential part of the smooth running of society and has an enormous influence upon the community…Your commitment is not a humiliation but a consecration!'[29]

For this reason, one may say that there is no job of greater or lesser importance: all are great if they are done lovingly and for the love of God. Work then acquires divine meaning, an offering that pleases God. Moreover, the seemingly humble and menial work of the household help has tremendous impact on the lives of people. Countless families owe a grand debt of gratitude to the unobtrusive but efficient support rendered by those who take on the difficult day-to-day adventure of caring for a home. Their wide and varied responsibilities run from looking after a grandmother who has to be taken out of bed, dressed and brought into the garden for some fresh air, to bathing and regularly changing the diapers of a two-month old baby. It takes a big heart to do all this, that is, a kindly, self-possessed soul who can still smile when asked to postpone a day-off or to work extra hours because there is a sick person to attend to or because visitors are expected.[30]

A mere "thank you" is not enough. Their valuable service requires financial remuneration that is not only just but also generous. Society ought to raise their professional status and offer them legal guarantees and security, spelling out their rights and their duties. Employers should treat them with every mark of respect and refinement. This also goes to say that

[29] John Paul II, *Address to the 10th Assembly of the APICOLF,* April 29, 1979.
[30] M. Sanchez, *op. cit.,* 36-37.

domestic helpers should be afforded the skills needed for the job. They need some general culture as well, that is suitable scientific and artistic training for housework and solid human and spiritual formation.

"(Good housekeeping) calls for women who are talented and who have a balanced and serene personality. Rudeness and unstable behavior will never do. A household helper must be alert, resourceful, and always eager to improve. She can not content herself with knowing how to make a French omelet and a few more dishes. That hardly makes her a professional cook. She has to know a lot more. Good cooking is an art that is difficult to master...A professional nanny should know the basics of child care and child psychology so that she can ably support her employer in forming and educating the children. She also has to know how to properly wash, iron and mend clothes, as well as to efficiently manage the market list and operate household appliances.[31]

It's no easy job. One needs persevering effort, the desire to improve, and a certain sense of professional accomplishment and self-worth which makes her worthy of a good paycheck, legal security, professional training, and human and spiritual formation.

"This is a great task, one would say almost a mission. For this, adequate preparation and maturity are necessary in order to be competent in the various household activities, to rationalize work and to get to know family psychology, the so-called pedagogy of fatigue which makes it possible to organize one's services better, and also to exercise the necessary educating function. It is a whole world, extremely

[31] M. Sanchez, *op. cit.,* 9-10.

important and precious, that every day opens up to your eyes and calls upon your sense of responsibility. I applaud, therefore, all women engaged in domestic activity and you, family collaborators, who offer your genius and your weariness for the good of the home!...

I would like to urge you to work above all with love in the families that employ you. We are living in difficult and complex times. Imposing, reprehensible phenomena, such as industrialization, urbanism, indiscriminate enculturation, precarious international relations, emotional instability, and the affectation of the intellect have caused confusion in families. With your presence, you can bring them serenity, peace, hope, joy, comfort, encouragement to do good, especially where there are elderly, sick and suffering persons, handicapped children, young people who are confused or who have been led astray. No law obliges you to smile! But you can make a gift of it. You can be the leaven of kindness in the family. Remember what St Paul wrote to the first Christians: *And whatever you do, in word or deed, do everything in the name of the Lord Jesus, giving thanks to God the Father through him* (Col 3:17). *Whatever your task, work heartily, as serving the Lord and not men, knowing that from the Lord you will receive the inheritance as your reward* (Col. 3:23-24). Love your work! Love the persons whom you are helping! For out of love and goodness shall spring your joy and your fulfillment...

May you be helped and comforted above all by Mary, who dedicated herself completely to the care of the family, and who set an example and shows us where true values lie."[32]

[32] John Paul II, *op cit.*

6

Chastity in Marriage

The word probably has a negative connotation, suggesting an attitude of repression or abstention—a forthright NO to sexuality. Those who think this way will see a contradiction in the term "chastity in marriage" because they take it to mean simple continence between spouses, a rejection of sex. The Christian message, however, is quite the contrary. It gives human sexuality its full human and supernatural meaning. It teaches us that chastity is positive, an affirmation of love. "Chastity is not merely continence but a decisive affirmation on the part of the will in love. It is a virtue that keeps love young in any state in life. There is a kind of chastity that corresponds to those who feel the awakening of physical maturity, and a kind of chastity that corresponds to those who are preparing for marriage; there is a chastity for those whom God calls to celibacy and a chastity for those who have been chosen by Him to live in the married state."[1]

[1] *Christ is Passing By* no. 25.

To better understand the expression, we can review some notions about human sexuality which, as we have seen, is not a purely biological reality but one that considers and embraces the core of one's personality. It is a basic dimension of the human personality, a mode of self-expression and a specific manner of loving and of communicating and living that love. Human sexuality refers not only to the physical characteristics of man and woman but also to their psychological and spiritual traits and the consequent manifestations of these as such. By their very differences, the two sexes complement each other and can fully carry out God's plan, which is the acceptance of the vocation to which one is called.[2]

Chastity is a good; it is a gift from God. "...for sexuality is an enrichment of the whole person—body, emotions and soul—and it manifests its inmost meaning in leading the person to the gift of self in love."[3] Its intrinsic end is love, a fruitful love or, more precisely, love as a gift and the acceptance of that gift. Since the relationship between the spouses is essentially a relationship of love, sexuality that is guided and integrated by love acquires a truly human character. It becomes "personal and truly human when it is integrated into the relationship of one person to another, in the mutual lifelong gift of a man and a woman."[4]

Hence the use of sex as a physical gift finds its truth and acquires full significance when it expresses the personal, lifetime exchange between a man and a woman.

[2] Cf. Congregation for Catholic Education, *Educative Guidelines On Human Love*, November 1, 1983, no. 4.

[3] FC 37.

[4] CCC 2337.

This integration of sexuality in the person and its consequent elevation to the supernatural order is made possible with the practice of a very specific virtue, which is that of chastity. Chastity is an essential part of the cardinal virtue of temperance, which moderates and guides the sensible appetites that accompany a person's vital functions. In a temperate person, reason governs the attraction to pleasure inherent to eating and to engaging in sexual activity. In other words, temperance ensures mastery over the instinct for pleasure, which in no way negates pleasure or suppresses one's ability to relish sensual delights but rather facilitates their reasonable and constructive enjoyment.

Man stands apart from other animals because he alone is capable of virtue (note that virtue means *strength*). Man alone can direct his appetites and govern them in accordance with reason. When he enjoys pleasurable goods, he does so in a manner that befits his dignity. However, if man gives free reign to his concupiscence, he ends up a slave to his passions, responding only to the prompting of his animal nature. Temperance ennobles the animal in man by subjecting it to reason, protecting man from the ever-present danger of turning into a beast. It is the virtue that enables him to live in accordance with his noble condition and dignity.

Chastity, in particular, moderates the sexual urge according to reason and directs it in a fitting manner to its proper end. It leads man to make use of sex only when circumstances ensure that sexual activity will be afforded its full human meaning, that is, intimately linked with the use of the intelligence and will, and respectful of its purpose in God's plan.

"If the person is not master of self—through the virtues and, in a concrete way, through chastity—he or she lacks that self-possession which makes self-giving possible. *Chastity is the spiritual power that frees love from selfishness and aggression.* To the degree that a person weakens chastity, his or her love becomes more and more selfish, that is, satisfying a desire for pleasure and no longer self-giving.

Chastity is the joyous affirmation of someone who knows how to live self-giving, free from any form of self-centered slavery. This presupposes that the person has learnt how to accept other people, to relate with them, while respecting their dignity in diversity. The chaste person is not self-centered, not involved in selfish relationships with other people. Chastity makes the personality harmonious. It matures it and fills it with inner peace. This purity of mind and body helps develop true self-respect and, at the same time, makes one capable of respecting others, because it makes one see in them persons to reverence insofar as they are created in the image of God and, through grace, are children of God, re-created by Christ *who called you out of darkness into his marvelous light*(1 Pet 2:9).[5]

It may seem difficult to be chaste. In fact, it is. This is why one resorts to certain means that entail effort but which, by experience, are most effective: rejecting glances, thoughts, desires, words, and actions that will endanger this virtue. "Chastity includes an *apprenticeship in self-mastery* which is a training in human freedom. The alternative is clear: either man governs his passions

---

[5] Pontifical Council for the Family, *The Truth and Meaning of Human Sexuality: Guidelines for Education within the Family*, 1995, nos. 16-17.

and finds peace, or he lets himself be dominated by them and becomes unhappy."[6] The battle nonetheless is tough and sometimes calls for heroism. Nevertheless, never forget that the grace of God is there as a buttress for one's weakness and misery. St Paul confirms it, saying, *I can do everything in him who strengthens me.*

Thus man and woman will feel the blessed pride and inner joy of victors in one of life's thousand battles. This is a real challenge. Thus we can properly refer to conjugal chastity when the virtue is practiced by married couples. Conjugal chastity is an important part of conjugal morality because it guides man's use of his God-given procreative power—a true participation in the divine creative power—to its true end.

Chastity therefore does not negate human sexuality or the procreative power. On the contrary, it is the virtue of one who recognizes the grandeur and dignity of sex and who wishes to defend it against possible abuses. Chastity not only bestows vitality to persons; it also gives them supernatural strength that will enable them to respect the authentic nature of human sexuality and to properly channel its power. Chastity renews one from within by making sex a genuine physical embodiment of conjugal love.

THE DIFFERENT ASPECTS OF CONJUGAL CHASTITY

We are now going to tackle the conditions that make sexual relationships in marriage fully human and hence worthy of receiving divine grace. They spell

[6] *CCC* 2339.

out in detail the various demands of chastity that spouses ought to live if their marriage is to be transformed into a divine path on earth, a sure means to personal satisfaction, and the basis of an effective family apostolate.

Among these conditions, the first which a married couple must bear in mind is that from the moment of marriage their sexual and emotional relationship is exclusive to themselves. This entails the practice of two virtues: *fidelity*, which means that physical self-giving takes place only between the spouses; and *generosity*, which leads spouses to give themselves to each other in a total way.

Fidelity

"A husband...who faithfully fulfills at each moment, in each new circumstance of his life, the duties of love and justice which he once took on, will always be just that much better a husband...It is difficult to keep this keen sense of loyalty constantly active, as it is always difficult to apply a principle to the changing realities of the contingent world. But it is the best defense against aging of the spirit, hardening of the heart, and stiffening of the mind."[7]

Husband and wife must know how to keep their pledge to each other. Their struggle to persevere in love must be constant and they must continuously renew the desire to preserve their unity and affection. They must always be willing to fight against tiredness, discouragement, and even life-long trials. These are

[7] *Conversations...* no. 1.

the consequences of an honest and noble sense of loyalty.

It is sad to see people, who after some years of married life, go about with their senses wide open, looking for new adventures, inviting temptations to infidelity and jeopardizing the stability of their marriage. What can be said of "divided" hearts? It is impossible to share one heart between two loves. Whoever wishes to venture into such an experiment can well remember Christ's words: *If a kingdom is divided against itself, that kingdom cannot stand. And if a house is divided against itself, that house will not be able to stand.*[8]

Infidelity always leads to unhappiness, sooner or later, in this life and in the next. It also shows a gross weakness of character, the absence of basic moral principles and an outlook that is degrading to human dignity. To be faithful may indeed be difficult at certain moments but it is never impossible to exercise if a person avoids occasions of sin and constantly renews his love. A yardstick of a person's worth is the capacity to be faithful to commitments and to be loyal to the person one has married with complete knowledge and freedom.

Matrimony is a union of love that demands the mutual and enduring self-surrender of the spouses. Husband and wife belong to each other and are no longer free to physically or emotionally give themselves to another. The virtue of fidelity defends the spouses against the temptation of taking back what they had pledged to each other on their wedding day.

———
[8] Mk 3:24.

"By joining yourselves together in matrimony in the presence of God, the Church, and your loved ones, you have solemnly promised to live mutual fidelity in all circumstances, whether favorable or adverse, along with love and mutual respect for as long as you live. Fidelity, love and respect are the fundamental attitudes that should be found at the base of all family life that is well-ordered. Through the sacrament (of marriage) they are elevated to a higher order. It is the Christian virtues that will enable you to form your own 'domestic church.' Following the example of Most Holy Mary and St Joseph, may your homes reflect the splendor of these virtues so that joy and peace may abide always in you."[9]

When true love—that is, love that has matured in sacrifice—inspires the union of the spouses, it is easy to live mutual fidelity because love that is constantly renewed is the best defense against betrayal. Unfortunately, not all married couples keep their love this way. Mutual fidelity is often endangered by neglect in cultivating love, the selfishness of one or the other partner, a poor spirit of sacrifice, and the absence of strong faith. These failings can break the physical, affective, or spiritual unity of the spouses.

Other dangers exist. There are couples who do love each other but still can put to risk their fidelity and consequent happiness. Think of what might happen if the husband or wife is absent for a prolonged period, probably driven by an upright desire to earn more for the family. Or when signs of aging inevitably or prematurely set in. Or when one starts to get too friendly with someone of the opposite

[9] John Paul II, *Address to Newlyweds*, January 3, 1979.

sex. Think of what vanity can lead to. The interest and attention can be very flattering, especially if these perks have been missing in one's marriage. Add to this an excessive sense of romance and an over-active imagination that brings one to long for new conquests and experiences.

Among men, the midlife crisis provokes anxiety about one's dwindling sex appeal; then come the momentary disappointments, family problems, frustration over the defects or attitudes of one's spouse, and even an intense social life that occasions excessive intimacy with other married couples. Many factors, all apparently trivial, may contribute to undermining mutual fidelity. Don't be fooled by these circumstances or be a naïve accomplice to such relationships.

Be brutally sincere and courageous from the very start—with one's self and with one's spouse. If one does not put up a good fight, any of these factors may even lead to the infidelity of the flesh—the sin of *adultery*, which gravely offends God, profanes the sacrament of marriage and violates the rights of the innocent spouse. *The husband should give to his wife her conjugal rights, and likewise the wife to her husband. For the wife does not rule over her own body, but the husband does; likewise the husband does not rule over his own body, but the wife does.*[10]

There is yet a worse danger which perhaps is usually afforded less attention: *the infidelity of the heart* which begins with subtle attitudes of mistrust, a real or apparent coldness, and the lack of dialogue between spouses. One feels misunderstood and unloved. As a consequence, one may innocently, though rather

[10] 1 Cor 7:3-4.

foolishly, start confiding in another person who can more readily offer consolation and relief. Affection for one's spouse therefore cools and can turn to another person. Such a situation may reach a point where husband and wife realize that they have become estranged even if they are physically living together. This can end in a break down of their union. Many couples find themselves in this situation and opt for an easy way out, an attitude marked by the absence of principles, values, nobility, and fighting spirit. Faced with a crisis, they desperately seek civil divorce because they find no remedy within the framework of Christian morals. They attempt a new marriage that is and will always be invalid in the eyes of God and the Church.

One can present many reasons in opposition God's will as regards the indissolubility of marriage—even of non-Catholic marriages. At bottom is a subtle temptation that couples do not always sincerely admit: that they want an easy solution, that they want to cop out. More often than not, they sing the same tune: "There's no point sticking to my wife. I am in love with another woman. Why can't I solve my problems in another way?"

Why? For the sake of fidelity. A love that used to be in your heart surely continues to be there. Such a love cannot vanish so easily unless you deliberately kill it and refuse to nurture it. Or perhaps you are not patient enough to wait for better days.

For the sake of fidelity to a common vocation to which you have been called by God so that you may form with your spouse one flesh and one soul.

For the sake of fidelity to the commitment you have freely contracted before God never to abandon your spouse: *Till death do us part*. So many tragedies and so much bitter loneliness result from having broken this pledge which all married couples must regard as sacred.

For the sake of fidelity to God who made marriage essentially indissoluble. God never makes mistakes. There are moments when we may not understand why, when it can be very hard to accept the facts. But if God has wanted things to be that way, then surely it is what's best for you. It is what befits human nature and harmonizes with the supernatural order of grace. It safeguards the happiness of husband and wife and it is best for the welfare of the children.

For the sake of fidelity to a sacrament which cannot be received again for as long as the other spouse is alive. It is a sacrament that can only bear fruits of holiness, peace, grace and godliness in the heart of this marriage that once took place before the altar. If you only knew the loss and the spiritual impoverishment that ensue from attempting to break this indissoluble bond.

For the sake of fidelity to the children who have every right to grow up with the parents who brought them into this world. The children have the right to experience the affection that their real parents alone can give. What a terrible life awaits children of broken homes. Their parents had yielded to the temptation of divorce because they had refused to fight adversity with all their might.

"What then can we do?" ask the many who are assailed by difficulties and fooled by facile answers to their desolation. The only logical answer: *Fight!*

Fight to overcome the obstacles. All marriages have their share of frictions and problems. You draw strength precisely from being faithful to this unbreakable commitment. There is no better or nobler way. How different this is from the cowardly and disloyal stance of those who immediately think of walking out in the face of the first serious difficulty.

Fight to overcome character differences and mutual grievances. Do so with charity that inspires understanding, forgives offenses and heals wounds. Seek peace in reconciliation and pardon, heeding the Apostle's advice: *Be angry but do not sin; do not let the sun go down on your anger, and give no opportunity to the devil.*[11] Difficulties can never be valid arguments against love.

Fight to rebuild the crumbling walls of the edifice of your marriage. Perhaps certain cracks were not repaired on time. Perhaps it got blasted from its very foundations. It does not matter. One can always resume the reconstruction, even if it means picking up the debris, one by one, with love and sacrifice.

Fight with the remaining strength that you and your spouse have, meager though it may be. Remember that charity will turn your weakness into strength.

Fight, trusting above all in God's grace. It will never be lacking in those who have received the sacrament of Matrimony, unless they themselves put obstacles to it. Christian spouses can be sure of this because God's word never fails.

Fight, contemplating that look in your spouse's eyes. Behind them lie desires or a deep sorrow that has never been said, probably because one is still licking the wounds of a badly injured sense of dignity and self-respect.

[11] Eph 4:26-27.

Fight, looking at the faces of your children. Their very silence proclaims that they would be the innocent victims of an irresponsible decision founded on so many "well-thought-out excuses."[12]

Fight from the start to the end, confident that nothing is hopeless. One can always start anew. Hope comes to anyone who calls on her persistently and without fear.

Fight, above all, against the slightest trace of infidelity. Use the means to promptly control the imagination whenever clouds of doubt or mistrust appear in the horizon. *An ounce of prevention is worth more than a pound of cure,* so an old saying goes. The first remedy is the constant effort to preserve and increase the love that led you to the altar in the first place. Do this with great delicacy and affection, with an understanding heart that never gives in to discouragement.

Another effective means is to practice prudence. Prudence calls for careful custody of the heart which can so often turn traitor when faced with persons other than your spouse. Married people should not go cruising like a cab driver on the look out for new passengers. Those who play around in this way ought to heed these wise words: "You give me the impression you are carrying your heart in your hands, as if you were offering goods for sale: Who wants it?"[13] The same advice applies to one who has given one's heart wholly to God as well as to one who has given one's heart to one's spouse. "Besides, when you opened one of the locks of your heart—which needs at least seven locks—isn't it true that more than once a cloud of

[12] *The Way* no. 21.
[13] *The Way* no. 146.

doubt remained over your soul? And you asked yourself, worried in spite of the purity of your intentions, 'Haven't I gone too far in my outward show of affection?' "[14]

We end but cannot help but add one more point for couples in crisis to reflect upon: " 'Oh, if only I had broken it off at the start!' you said to me. May you never have to repeat that belated exclamation."[15]

Conjugal Generosity

We have said that both spouses have to pool their efforts so that chastity may inspire the sexual act and thus direct it to its proper end. The marital act is not a selfish act because through it husband and wife engage in a most intimate form of exchange and communication. Not long ago, the Italian newspapers bore a news item about a man who murdered his wife after being married to her for many years. The reason? *She always pulled the blankets to her side of the bed!* Does not a similar situation happen in many marriages where one of the partners, in the use of sex as well as in other areas of marital living, is only concerned about one's pleasure without considering in any way the needs of the other?

A husband acts selfishly in those intimate moments with his wife when he does not allow her the freedom of heart and spirit proper to an interpersonal relationship and which so enriches both spouses. A husband who behaves this way treats his wife unfairly and

[14] *Ibid.*, no. 161.
[15] *Ibid.*, no. 167.

contradicts the demands of authentic conjugal chastity. He subjects her to serious psychological tension and may even push her to give in to possible temptations. Similarly, a woman's vanity can lead her to give herself to her husband only because she wants to feel desired. The woman should know that this coquetry of sorts, a narcissistic hankering for attention, is not at all upright or pure. She behaves unchastely because by playing "hard-to-get" she willfully manipulates her husband into giving her more attention. The use of sex thus becomes impure because it is removed from the context of total love and made to serve a selfish end.[16]

One also fails to be generous in living conjugal chastity when one demands for the marital act even if, for some valid reason, it would be burdensome, unpleasant or annoying to one's partner. The more serious offense, however, would be to deny a reasonable request, since both spouses are bound to render the marriage debt whenever it is asked for: It is an obligation of justice and of love. In this sense, husband and wife no longer have rights over their bodies.[17]

What, then, are the limits? Up to what point is one obliged to give in to the request of the other? What circumstances justify refusing the marriage debt?

[16] Cf. Jouvenroux, *Testimonio sobre el amor humano.*

[17] *But because of the temptation to immorality, each man should have his own wife and each woman her own husband. The husband should give to his wife her conjugal rights, and likewise the wife to her husband. For the wife does not rule over her own body, but the husband does; likewise the husband does not rule over his own body, but the wife does. Do not refuse one another except perhaps by agreement for a season, that you may devote yourselves to prayer; but then come together again, lest Satan tempt you through lack of self-control.* (1 Cor 7: 2-5).

Before answering, we must consider that these duties of justice have to be moderated by prudence and inspired by charity. One should avoid the cold "I-have-the-right-to-it" attitude. Simply said, a married couple fulfill their duty in this regard when neither of them refuses the other when the marriage debt is reasonably asked for—even if he or she may not feel like doing it. Refusal would even be a serious offense when one foresees that this would push the other spouse to be incontinent and unfaithful.

On the other hand, refusal is justifiable if the request is made unreasonably, as when one asks for it in a state of drunkenness, or if both spouses have previously agreed to live continence, or if serious problems would ensue due to illness or physical or moral exhaustion. When sexual intercourse would only cause serious discomfort to the spouse, it is the duty of the other to abstain from it out of love and delicacy for one's partner.

This is a manifestation of disinterested love and a spirit of sacrifice. For one cannot call the conjugal act an act of love when it is imposed on the other without considering one's present condition or legitimate desires. In this case, right moral order does not govern or inspire the spousal relationship.

Generosity is vital to conjugal relationships and to the overall moral behavior of the spouses. It is also a source of their happiness and of holiness and of peace and cheerfulness in the home. People who are truly in love should frequently ask themselves whether they are generous or whether, in a more or less hidden way, they allow themselves to be led by love of comfort and selfishness. They should check whether they are thinking too much of themselves or are only seeking their own satisfaction. For such attitudes are what makes people unhappy. On the other hand, total self surrender brings happiness—a true foretaste of heaven on earth.[18]

The Role of the Spirit:
Moderation and Delicacy

Conjugal chastity is the measure of the humanity as well as of the divinity of the husband-wife relationship. One cannot ignore the role of the human spirit here. By nature, man cannot be fixated on and thereby stagnate in the superficial pleasures of the flesh. Man cannot but seek the deepest meaning of love in everything. This is why the physical union of the spouses ought to be a symbol and at the same time a vehicle for their union of hearts. The language of their bodies should signify a greater degree of spiritual unity, a physical expression of their union of soul.

The virtue of chastity—that is, the supernatural virtue infused by God into the soul and which elevates the human virtue of chastity—leads spouses to savor their intimate moments not just on the level of physical enjoyment but also as an experience of love which is blessed by God. God is pleased when spouses turn their sexual union into an act of genuine human love, for here the role of the soul is just as important as that of the body. In these moments, husband and wife are guided above all by the spiritual—that is, rational—

18 Cf. *Christ is Passing By* no. 24.

values. This does not mean, however, that spouses "disembody" their love. Far from it, they heighten the spiritual, human and supernatural content of their sexual union. Such is the end that the virtue of conjugal chastity.

Married couples must therefore take care of fostering this virtue. It keeps carnal desires within their proper limits and moderates the otherwise excessive arousal of the sensitive part of man. Without chastity, the road is open to lust and to the darkening of reason to the higher values and to divine realities. When one excessively prizes the values of the flesh, he unconsciously loses an appreciation for the values of the spirit. For *the unspiritual man does not receive the gifts of the Spirit of God, for they are folly to him, and he is not able to understand them because they are spiritually discerned.*[19] Once the preoccupation with pleasure takes hold of the mind, marriage becomes a common life of selfishness and sensuality.

However, when a man strives to live up to his dignity, he exerts constant effort to be in control of his actions and to make them more humane. Which means that one's acts are guided by reason, impregnated by human affection, and inspired by ideals and moral convictions. In this way, one's actions will always be guided by reason and never degenerate into mere instinctive reactions. It may be true that man's biological functions are largely similar to those of some animals. Take one's digestive processes: Like those of brutes, these lie beyond a man's control. Nevertheless a human being normally refuses to be animal-like in his eating habits and behavior, in his reactions to gastro-

[19] 1 Cor 2:14.

nomic stimuli, and in his general attitude to food. A human being's way of eating shows a marked contrast, externally as well as internally, to that of an animal because he is endowed with the reason and the will to moderate, control and direct his actions.

The same idea applies to a human being's sexual activity. Although some aspects of human sexuality show similarities to those of brute animals, others fall within the realm of conscious activity and therefore ought to be imbued with genuine human content. This is achieved when the licit use of sex is accompanied by self-control, moderation and refinement. And chastity is the virtue that guides the spouses in the use of sex; it gives their licit and noble acts a new, supernatural dimension that makes them holy in the eyes of God. In their sexual relations, spouses must control their appetites with reason enlightened by faith. A person is more deeply and keenly affected by sexual pleasure than by any other bodily delight. This is why when one allows himself to be completely taken by it, disorder is likely to break loose in a more vehement way. For this reason, the sexual drive is more difficult to moderate than any of the other passions. Hence, spouses ought to help one another acquire the self-mastery that will enable them to keep their sexual appetite within proper bounds; for once passion is given free reign, it easily enslaves a person. No wonder people totally taken up by sex think that it is utopian to practice sexual continence when this is called for in certain periods, such as a temporary separation of husband and wife, or when having more children would pose serious difficulties, or when either spouse is sick.

How is the mastery of the sexual drive of spouses to be understood? Let us first forestall any misunderstanding about this. Self-control may be misunderstood in two ways: First, to think that it is simply a matter of reducing the number of times one engages in the sexual act, the same way one tries to cut down on smoking. The other misconception is to try to stifle the intensity of the pleasure experienced during sexual intercourse. Neither one is right. Self-mastery consists in the effort to avoid uncontrolled, irrational and inhuman behavior. It is to strike a balance so that love, in its physical expression, becomes more human each time, more imbued with spiritual values, less influenced by selfishness, and more attentive to the needs and reasonable requests of the other. It is to gradually turn sexual intercourse into a more perfect physical expression of profound love, and not an escape valve for instinct. It puts a check on obsession and considers sex as a suitable help for the couple to grow in authentic love. It transcends simple sensual delight and transforms the union of bodies into a fusion of spirits, affections and ideals.

Obviously, self-mastery is a long, difficult and maturing process. It reflects the husband and wife's idea of conjugal love as well as their attitudes toward other situations in life. Thus if at other moments of the day a couple is habitually given to excess and disproportionate anger and if they are bullheaded and unyielding to each other, then it will be very hard to instill their sexual relations with the human and supernatural qualities of authentic love.

Self-mastery in one's sexual relations is not so much a question of reducing the amount of pleasure as in fighting the temptation to indulge one's self without any consideration for one's spouse. It is the effort not to succumb to a materialistic attitude that leads one to prize bodily pleasure above any other good. Once more, we see the role of chastity in preserving what is most human and precious in marital relationships. It brings into play the virtue of charity, the highest and the noblest Christian virtue.

What are the fruits of controlling the sexual drive? "To dominate instinct by means of one's reason and free will undoubtedly requires ascetical practices, so that the affective manifestations of conjugal life may observe the correct order, in particular with regard to the observance of periodic continence. Yet this discipline which is proper to the purity of married couples, far from harming conjugal love, rather confers on it a higher human value. It demands continual effort yet, thanks to its beneficent influence, husband and wife fully develop their personalities, being enriched with spiritual values.

Such discipline bestows upon family life fruits of serenity and peace, and facilitates the solution of other problems; it favors attention for one's partner, helps both parties to drive out selfishness, the enemy of true love; and deepens their sense of responsibility. By its means, parents acquire the capacity of having a deeper and more efficacious influence in the education of their offspring; little children and youths grows up with a just appraisal of human values, and in the serene and harmonious development of their spiritual and sensitive faculties."[20]

[20] *HV* 21.

Avoid Any Cheapening of Love

The Second Vatican Council, particularly conscious of the problem of man and his calling, states that the conjugal union, the biblical *una caro*, can be understood and fully explained only by *recourse to the values of the 'person' and of 'gift.'* Every man and every woman fully realizes himself or herself through the sincere gift of self. For spouses, the moment of conjugal union constitutes a very particular expression of this. It is then that a man and woman, in the 'truth' of their masculinity and femininity, become a mutual gift to each other. All married life is a gift; but this becomes most evident when the spouses, in giving themselves to each other in love, bring about that encounter which makes them one flesh (Gen 2:24)."[21]

It must be borne in mind that sexuality is subject to natural laws that have been clearly enunciated by Christian morals and that the observance of these laws is the object of the virtue of chastity. According to these norms, it is not lawful for spouses to employ every means available to stimulate pleasure. The mutual exchange between spouses must be highlighted by the virtue of chastity such that, in all things, husband and wife conduct themselves in accordance with the law of God and nature. Nowadays, tons of literature that claim scientific soundness end up tainting the marital relationship with unnatural techniques and devices that are well-calculated to satisfy erotic desires. Their use better serves the purpose of brothels (which could very well have been their origin) than that of the noble, decent and normal expression of love between

[21] John Paul II, *Letter to Families*, 1994, no. 12.

Christian spouses. It is not difficult to see why such practices are a perversion of love.[22]

But the question arises: Where do we draw the limits of conjugal chastity during the physical expressions of love? The following general rule can be given. In marital relationships, God permits everything which is ordained either to procreation or to expressing pure conjugal love in a manner that does not hinder procreation. The conjugal act—along with the concomitant sexual pleasure—is lawful and clean as long as no obstacle is placed to its natural end.[23] Neither does it cease to be lawful even if, for no fault on the part of husband or wife, the act is foreseen to be infecund. It will always be an expression of their love and a means to strengthen their union.

As for the actions which accompany sexual union (e.g., the kisses, embraces and caresses) and which

[22] "Many people think that once a couple are married, it is lawful to pursue pleasure by all means, including those intricate methods that are clearly perverted. Indeed, they do not realize that the indiscriminate use of every means to intensify pleasure is, in itself, a perversion...Even among the young who show signs of being very Christian, there are some who are sorely ignorant about conjugal morals and who go by the rudimentary rule that outside marriage everything is prohibited, while within marriage everything is permitted..." (J. Leclerq, *op. cit.*, 224-225).

[23] "The actions within marriage by which the couple are united intimately and chastely are noble and worthy ones. Expressed in a manner which is truly human, these actions promote that mutual self-giving by which spouses enrich each other with a joyful and a ready will...Hence, the acts themselves which are proper to conjugal love and which are exercised in accord with genuine human dignity must be honored with great reverence." (Vatican Council II, Pastoral Constitution *GS* 49 & 50).

prepare for and complement the act in a more or less immediate way, these are morally licit because they are objectively and intrinsically connected with the marital act. This holds even if the couple do not intend to engage in sexual intercourse, provided they avoid the proximate danger of complete satisfaction. And even if climax were to be reached in a totally unforeseen way, there would be no sin as long as they did not willfully seek it.

In short, it is a question of following the natural laws of love. These laws permit spouses to express their love in countless ways, drawing strength from the inexhaustible riches of the human heart and without having to resort to artificial devices that stimulate erotic pleasure. The intimate moments shared by the spouses can remain fresh and new even without such illicit means because the joy they experience goes beyond the superficial delights of the flesh: It involves the nobler values of generous self-giving. This sense of totality in their love shuns monotony and ensures the constant renewal of their mutual affection and self-surrender.

Openness to Life[24]

Human life is sacred from the moment of conception. Both God and the married couple are involved in bringing new life to the world. God makes the human spouses share in his creative work. Man shares in God's being and power chiefly through his intelligence and procreative power; hence it is crucial that man should use these gifts in the proper manner. He must not use them capriciously but in accordance with the will of the One who gave them to him. This sacred gift must be received with the respect due a precious item: one is careful not to destroy its meaning and purpose. In the same way, husband and wife must not violate the gift to procreate while engaging in the intimacy of their love and fidelity to each other. In other words, spouses should respect the laws of the generative

[24] The topics that we shall deal with in the following sections have been and continue to be the subject of heated discussion in various publications. We are going to tackle the subject matter from the same perspective: That marriage is a path to sanctity and heroic virtue, and a generous exercise in loving God. Our basic assumptions have always been the supernatural transcendence of the Catholic faith and our obedience to the Church. This is why we quote much from texts of the Magisterium, finding in them a valid and reasonable exposition of why generous and self-sacrificing love is essential to seeking human perfection as well as spiritual fulfillment. We absolutely accept the authority of the Vicar of Christ and recognize the right of the Church to authentically interpret the natural law and apply the divine precepts to the moral conduct of married couples. We opted not to delve into other related aspects, such as the economic and the social perspectives, because they fall outside our scope of interest. Our primary concern here is the Christian's personal relationship with God and with his own family—what we believe to be every person's starting point as he freely and responsibly tries to work out the problems posed by society and the historical circumstances that he is presently living. In this task, a person is inspired to selflessly work for the welfare of others, guided by a hierarchy of values where supernatural ideals holds primacy over the human, even when sometimes the two seem to clash. We make detailed references to the biological aspect of the issue, which we shall always consider within the framework of morality, because one of the authors of this book is a medical doctor who has had long years of pedagogical and scientific experience in marriage counseling.

process being, as such, not arbiters but stewards and custodians of God's master plan. Just as man does not have absolute dominion over his body, so too and with more reason does he hold no such dominion over his generative faculties, whose intrinsic purpose is to raise up new life and whose origin and end is God himself.

Married couples personally assume the transcendent mission to transmit and educate human life, bearing in mind that they are cooperating in God's love and are, in a sense, "interpreters" of this love.[25] And since it is God's will to bestow on spouses this special participation in his creative work, making them collaborators of his love, they ought to use this power with heartfelt gratitude to the Creator, keenly aware of the confidence he has shown them. It is also natural that they should carry out the task lovingly, with all the effort and sacrifices required to live up to their Lord's expectations. From here springs not only a sense of human and Christian gratitude, but also the responsibility to fulfill the duty to beget children.

This idea must constantly influence the spouses' attitude towards the noble and divine mission that has been entrusted to them. This is why they must make sure that selfishness should never get the upper hand in their married life. This is also why they ensure that this joyful obligation to bring new life to the world is always guided by sound moral principles. It is therefore logical that Christian parents should want to have many children. Still, "The great danger for family life in the midst of any society whose idols are pleasure, comfort and independence, lies in the fact that people close their hearts and become selfish. The fear

[25] Cf. *GS* 49-50.

of making permanent commitments can change the mutual love of husband and wife into two loves of self—two loves existing side by side until they end in separation."[26]

Large Families

In the section that touched on responsible parenthood, we said that the Church does not indiscriminately force Christian couples to have more children than what they can actually afford and educate. It is the parents who decide on the number of children they should have. However, this decision is backed up by serious and mature reflection, knowing that both spouses will have to render God an account of how generous they had been to him in this matter. Bearing this in mind, we would like to expound on the positive side of having a large family.

There are many good reasons to praise those who, realizing the inestimable value of having many children, freely and without fear of sacrifice, open their homes to the children God wishes to send them. They probably realize that it is their mission on Earth to raise a large family and that shirking this obligation would be a serious sin of omission.

Following the tradition of the Church, the Second Vatican Council renders nothing but praise to spouses who, in fulfilling their God-given duty, "with a gallant heart, and with wise and common deliberation,

[26] John Paul II, *Homily at Capital Hill*, Washington, October 7, 1979.

undertake to bring up suitably even a relatively large family."[27] It is to families such as these that the following praise of Sacred Scripture is addressed: *Your wife will be like a fruitful vine within your house; your children will be like olive shoots around your table. Lo thus shall the man be blessed who fears the Lord.*[28] Children are a real blessing from the Lord. This is why when, for no serious and objective reason, spouses refuse to have children—many children—they show that they have lost that strong, innate instinct to perpetuate themselves. They have become adulterated, as it were, allowing selfishness to suppress or even crush out this noble inclination.

It is true that many times spouses will have to sacrifice their desire to have many children because of a real inability to feed, educate and bring up a large family. A costly sacrifice no doubt, but one that is well made, provided it is inspired by the demands of responsible parenthood and lived in accordance with the norms of chastity. On the other hand, it is not easy to understand why some couples who have enough resources to support more children (and we are not only referring to couples with money to spare) refuse to carry out this marvelous ideal.

One may ask whether they have lost the natural desire to have children, the fruit of man's highest calling to parenthood, or if their love is genuine and strong, as all fecund love is by nature. Or is it perhaps that hedonism has killed the deepest and most normal aspirations of the human heart, for such an attitude is

---

[27] John Paul II, *Address*, November 3, 1979.
[28] Ps 128:3-4.

proper to the mean and the cowardly. Sad to say, many young couples sustain a narrow-minded and pusil-lanimous attitude toward bearing children. They tend to fear the worst for the children who are yet to come: "What kind of life awaits them?" "One can never be sure of the future." "We don't want to bring children into a world that will only make them suffer." Such are the reasons of the selfish and the small-minded.

On the other hand, there are magnanimous hearts who, freed of egoism, realize the value of a large family and savor the joy it brings. They experience the wonders of a fruitful marriage even it would mean inevitable sacrifice, but a sacrifice that affords them training in the virtues of self-denial and generosity. There is no doubt that parents of large families must forego many good and noble desires. Mothers have to undergo more frequently the burdens and limitations of pregnancy; the rest of the family, too, must constantly adjust their lifestyle to accommodate every new baby that is born. Nevertheless, everything is compensated for by the blessings children bring—the deep and genuine joy of their presence.

"To maintain a joyful family life requires much sacrifice from both the parents and the children... Decisions about the number of children and the sacrifices to be made for them must not be made taking into account only one's comfort and peace of mind. Reflecting upon the matter before God, helped by the graces drawn from the sacrament of marriage, and guided by the teachings of the Church, parents should remember that to deny their children certain comforts or material benefits is certainly less serious than to deprive them of brothers and sisters who will help them grow in humanity and appreciate the beauty of life in all its stages and in all its variety."[29]

The joy of a large family is above all a moral joy that one can already appreciate with a minimum of uprightness and good will. One can never understand it purely from a material or economic perspective. We can adduce the thousand reasons to be happy about the difficult and demanding task of having children, and many at that, if the circumstances should allow it. Here are some of them:

Children are the glory of their parents. Hardly anywhere else can parents find a greater, nobler and more selfless joy than to hear their children's innocent laughter and to watch them grow by their side. Parents sacrifice themselves for their children's welfare. They regard their children's good as their own because their children have become an integral part of their lives. Parents perpetuate themselves physically and spiritually in their children. They live on, as it were, in them. Without doubt, the blessings that children bring contribute to the happiness of the parents.

Children are their parent's constant stimulus to want to be better persons. They become capable of things that they had never done before. They work harder, bear greater trials and find themselves overcoming great obstacles. There can be no better reason for a person to make heroic sacrifices. This is why spouses who purposely deprive themselves of offspring or who "stop at two" live a common life of selfishness, which is more dangerous than the selfishness of a single person because it is subtle and can easily pass itself off as love.

[29] J. Leclerq, *op. cit.*, 259.

Children are the best seal of conjugal love because they forge a new bond between husband and wife. Children are their common fruit and nothing else can embody their union in a more perfect way. Parents realize that if there is anything that requires more unity and concord between them, it is the formation of their children. Many squabbling couples have found harmony and reconciliation by giving the best of themselves to the education of their children.

Children are their parents' pride because the ineffable fulfillment of man is to form another man. All the wealth of man's participation in God's creative power is seen when he begets another human being whom one can very well call his own. Husband and wife see themselves in their children; they feel that they live on in them.

Finally, from the supernatural standpoint, parents play an awesome role in the divine task of *increasing the number of God's children on earth*. God wants more men to be born, not only to fill up the earth but also to worship him, know him, love him, and be with him in heaven. This hardly make sense from a purely human and material point of view, for only the eyes of faith can discover the incalculable wisdom of these words. One then will understand that the duty to transmit human life is not understood only in worldly terms; it has a bearing on the eternal destiny of man.

Still, a question remains: In the light of the population issue, can the State oblige married couples to limit their number of children? Bearing in the mind that such a decision is a personal thing between husband and wife, clearly, State pressure in this regard is unlawful. Although the State may deem it necessary to adopt extraordinary measures to avoid any perceived negative effects of overpopulation, such measures can only be lawful if they adhere to the demands of moral law and respect the just freedom of the spouses.

State leaders ought to be aware of their moral responsibilities in this area. It would be wrong for them to succumb to the temptation of limiting population growth through policies that transgress the personal freedom of consciences. One cannot speak of human dignity without taking into account a person's inalienable right to marriage and procreation. In the end, the decision as regards the number of children belong solely to the parents who accept their duties to God, to themselves, to the offspring that they have already brought to the world, and to the community of which they form part. But in so doing couples must follow the dictates of conscience, guided by God's laws which are authentically interpreted and upheld by those who trust in Him. Thus, any government or public authority that tries to curtail the freedom of spouses in deciding the matter for themselves violates personal human dignity. It is likewise unjust and unlawful for international bodies to grant economic aid to poorer countries on the condition that these should adopt population control programs, including sterilization and abortion.

A government that is truly concerned about fostering social justice and the public good has many means to create employment, multiply opportunities for development and put the benefits of progress at the service of the people. It is a government that trusts in the potential and resources of tomorrow's citizens and future workforce and does not see them merely as an extra burden. It is always therefore a more just and magnanimous move to think of ways to increase the amount of food served at table rather than to forcibly reduce the number of mouths to feed.

Christian statesmen can contribute to a positive population policy by fostering well-thought-of educational programs that promote the family and which keep to the moral law and respect the freedom of persons. Such problems and issues are best tackled by a keen mind and a generous heart. In this way, one can formulate truly human and truly Christian solutions. One cannot keep on passing the buck to Divine Providence to set aright mistakes due to incompetent governance, a poor sense of social justice, selfish monopolization, or unpardonable laziness. Man, too, should count on personal effort and sacrifice to uplift the social and economic conditions of his own family and of his country.

Related Issues

To complete the explanation of conjugal morality, we would like to present some teachings of the Church regarding the fecundity of marriage as well as the moral norms laid down by the Magisterium concerning contraceptives and periodic continence.

Following closely the papal teachings, we said that the union of love between spouses must, for natural and supernatural reasons, find external expression in the children; hence, it is not lawful for couples to block the wellsprings of life. In order to further clarify any more doubts regarding this very important matter, the ordinary Magisterium of the Church has established, expressed and interpreted a number of norms to guide and inspire conjugal relationships so that the use of marriage may always be in keeping with the natural and divine-positive law.

In these times of intense ecological activism, where respect for nature figures as the preeminent battle cry, it is difficult to understand how and why artificial methods and unnatural procedures have gained much ground on such a natural and extremely personal terrain as the generation of human life. Does not the substitution of the spouses' common effort at self-mastery and self-renunciation (for the sake of the other) with mere technique indicate a deterioration of what is most noble in man? Do we not realize that human nature is subordinated to morality? Has anyone measured how the rejection of a child—now a rampant practice—has a bearing on the psychology of its parents, who by nature bear the desire for offspring? Do we not realize how much this affects the future of society? What can we say about the kind of sex education offered to the young? It encourages rather than protects them against seeking immediate, selfish pleasure, oblivious of the responsibilities of conjugal love and procreation.[30] What principles are there for married couples to hang on to?

First, Catholic morality teaches that every marital act must be open to the transmission of life. Spouses who deprive their union of the procreative gift act unlawfully and violate natural law.

[30] Cf. John Paul II, *Address to the CLER and the FIDAP.*

"It is precisely by moving from *an integral vision of man and of his vocation, not only his natural and earthly, but also his supernatural and eternal vocation* that Paul VI affirmed that the teaching of the Church *is founded upon the inseparable connection, willed by God and unable to be broken by man on his own initiative, between the two meaning of the conjugal act: the unitive meaning and the procreative meaning...*

When couples, by means of recourse to contraception, separate these two meaning that God the Creator has inscribed in the being of man and woman and in the dynamism of their sexual communion, they act as 'arbiter' of the divine plan and 'manipulate' and degrade human sexuality—and with it, themselves and their married partner—by altering the value of 'total' self-giving. Thus the innate language that expresses the total reciprocal self-giving of husband and wife is overlaid, through contraception, by an objectively contradictory language, namely, that of not giving oneself totally to the other. This leads not only to a positive refusal to be open to life but also to a falsification of the inner truth of conjugal love, which is called upon to give itself in personal totality."[31]

Now, if due to serious reasons adduced by a well-formed Christian conscience, a couple agrees to limit their number of children, then they must keep in mind two things: the lawfulness of limiting the number of births and the lawfulness of the means employed to do so. Assuming that their reasons are medical, eugenic, economic or social in nature, it is lawful to limit the

---

[31] John Paul II, *FC* 32.

number of new births either for a fixed period or even indefinitely. This decision must be made in conscience by both spouses who are, therefore, personally answerable to God for their choice. And once they have decided, it is up to them to study the methods to use because from the moral point of view, there is a clear-cut difference between the natural birth control methods and those that are artificial and, therefore, immoral. For a Christian, the answer cannot be based simply on "which method is more effective." It has to be grounded on serious reflection—a moral judgment included—on the dictates of the natural law.

Contraceptive Methods

We refer to all methods of birth control which, because they are incompatible with the divine law, have been condemned by the Church as morally illicit.

The first is **abortion**, which will never be lawful as a method of birth control even if one resorts to it for therapeutic reasons. Life must be respected at all stages of its development. A child must be protected from the moment of conception; thus abortion and infanticide are abominable crimes and as such are subject to canonical legislation. In the Code of Canon Law, the Church classifies abortion as a grave crime subject to a serious penalty, which is the excommunication of anyone who somehow participate in it, including the spouses, the attending doctors and nurses, and those who advised the couple to resort to it. [32]

---

[32] Cf. *Code of Canon Law,* can. 1398.

Direct sterilization of either spouse, whether temporary or definitive, is likewise forbidden. The definitive sterilization of a man (**vasectomy**) or a woman (**ligation of the Fallopian tubes**) is a sin against nature because it mutilates a person's vital functions. No power on earth can claim absolute control over a human being's organs or vital functions. Only God is the Lord of life and only he can dispose of it. If man does not have unlimited dominion over his body, with more reason can he not have unlimited dominion over his generative faculties since their natural purpose is to beget life, of which God is the principle and end.

This sin against the integrity of the human body has inevitable repercussions on conjugal chastity. A person who has been voluntarily sterilized and who has not sincerely repented of this sin and made reparation for it, can render his sexual relations illicit. What could have been a married couple's expression of love and a path towards generous self-giving and holiness would then become a vehicle for sin and a road that would slowly lead them away from God.

As for methods of temporary sterilization, we have the **oral contraceptives**—more commonly known as the Pill—and the **injectable contraceptives**. These are chemical compounds of estrogens and gestagens that momentarily prevent ovulation and, hence, induce fertility in the woman. The Magisterium of the Church regards these methods as anti-natural and therefore sinful because they artificially render a woman infertile and therefore directly impair the very essence of the marital act. Moreover, besides preventing ovulation—which is never 100% guaranteed—these contraceptive methods have other effects that are hardly spoken about. One side effect is that these can alter the motility of the Fallopian tubes, thus affecting the velocity of the fertilized egg as it makes its way through the tube. When the fertilized egg finally reaches the uterus, it is unable to implant itself and is subsequently expelled. The result is abortion, plain and simple.[33] Another side effect occurs in the endometrium, which is the inner lining of the uterus. Some contraceptives render it impossible for the embryo to be implanted, thus again resulting in abortion. These two effects lead us to conclude that there are grave biological and moral consequences to taking contraceptive pills. A woman who has been on the Pill for months is more like to have had an induced abortion.[34]

Catholic teachings likewise decry any act immediately before, during or after sexual intercourse that would purposely make procreation impossible. These include all artificial means—chemical (**spermicides, douches**), mechanical (**condoms, IUDs**) or physical (**withdrawal**)—that would prevent conception. Due to its widespread use, the intra-uterine device (**IUD**) deserves special mention. This device, which comes in different shapes and materials, is inserted into the uterus to prevent the implantation of the embryo, clearly proving its abortifacient function.

"It must be added that the widespread practice of artificial contraception also leads to abortion, for both

_____

[33] Cf. Juan Jiménez Vargas and G. Lopez Garcia, *Abortion and Contraceptives*, University of Navarre, Pamplona, Spain, 1973.

[34]*Ibid.*

methods, at certainly different levels, follow the same line of thought, which is the fear of children, a rejection of life, a lack of respect for the act or fruit of the union between man and woman which is so willed by the Creator of nature."[35]

If, despite knowing the above-mentioned biological and moral consequences, a couple—either by mutual agreement or with one partner inconsiderately imposing his or her preferences on the other—persist in using contraceptive devices, they must realize that their marriage is going off-track. Instead of becoming a path to happiness, fruitfulness, sanctity and personal salvation, their union becomes a direct defiance to God. Moreover, husband and wife end up regarding each other as accomplices in their pride and selfishness and so put their love in jeopardy. A train of other consequences ensues: emotional instability, infidelity, disharmony in the home, and despondency in the children.[36]

---

[35] John Paul II, *Address to the CLER*, November 3, 1979.

[36] "Upright men can even better convince themselves of the solid grounds on which the teaching of the Church in this field is based, if they care to reflect upon the consequences of methods of artificial birth control. Let them consider, first of all, how wide and easy a road would thus be opened up towards conjugal infidelity and the general lowering of morality. Not much experience is needed in order to know human weakness, and to understand that men—especially the young, who are so vulnerable on this point—have need of encouragement to be faithful to the moral law, so that they must not be offered some easy means of eluding its observance. It is also to be feared that man, growing used to the employment of anti-conceptive practices, may finally lose respect for the woman and, no

Periodic Continence

Before closing this section on conjugal chastity, we ought to comment on periodic continence or the use of sex only during a woman's infertile periods. We are not so much concerned about the physiological aspect of the matter (which falls outside the scope of this work), as with its moral and ascetical implications. The Magisterium of the Church has always clarified the lawfulness of periodic continence, affirming that married couples, for serious motives, may be dispensed from the obligation to collaborate with God in begetting new lives. These serious, important and grave reasons, which may be medical, eugenic, or socio-economic in nature, may exempt some spouses from engaging in the marital act for a long time or, if necessary, for the whole duration of their marriage. In these cases, the Church teaches that it is licit to consider the natural rhythms immanent in the generative functions. A couple may therefore engage in the marital act only during a woman's infertile periods, thus regulating the number of births without violating the aforementioned moral principles.

Some may conclude that the Church contradicts herself when she permits this method of regulating births while condemning others which have the same

longer caring for her physical and psychological equilibrium, may come to the point of considering her as a mere instrument of selfish enjoyment, and no longer as his respected and beloved companion. Let it be considered also that a dangerous weapon would thus be placed in the hands of those public Authorities who take no heed of moral exigencies." (Paul VI, *HV* 17).

objective. John Paul II, however, dispels doubts in this regard:

"When, instead, by means of recourse to periods of infertility, the couple respect the inseparable connection between the unitive and procreative meanings of human sexuality, they are acting as 'ministers' of God's plan and they 'benefit from' their sexuality according to the original dynamism of 'total' self-giving, without manipulation or alteration.

In the light of the experience of many couples and of the data provided by the different human sciences, theological reflection is able to perceive and is called to study further *the difference, both anthropological and moral*, between contraception and recourse to the rhythm of the cycle: it is a difference which is much wider and deeper than is usually thought, one which involves in the final analysis two irreconcilable concepts of the human person and of human sexuality. The choice of the natural rhythms involves accepting the cycle of the person, that is the woman, and thereby accepting dialogue, reciprocal respect, shared responsibility and self-control. To accept the cycle and to enter into dialogue means to recognize both the spiritual and corporal character of conjugal communion, and to live personal love with its requirement of fidelity. In this context the couple comes to experience how conjugal communion is enriched with those values of tenderness and affection which constitute the inner soul of human sexuality, in its physical dimension also. In this way sexuality is respected and promoted in its truly and fully human dimension, and is never 'used' as an 'object' that, by breaking the personal unity of body and soul, strikes at God's creation itself at the level of the deepest interaction of nature and person."[37]

The lawfulness therefore of recourse to periodic continence is not absolute but qualified by the existence of serious, important and grave reasons. These may be medical in nature, as for instance, a sickness that may endanger the life of the mother or that of the unborn child. Then again it may be eugenic, as in the possibility of bearing psychologically impaired or retarded offspring. There are also grave economic reasons, which would be the gross lack of means to feed and educate more children, or extreme social conditions, such as poor housing or unjust population laws. If such reasons do not exist, then recourse to periodic continence would still be unlawful. It would be even a graver offense to practice periodic continence so that one may live more comfortably, enjoy a better financial status, acquire more material amenities, or simply have more peace of mind by shirking the difficulties that raising children entail. For these reasons, spouses are advised to be prudent and seek sound advice in applying the papal teachings to their specific situation. It is the teaching authority of the Church that interprets the law of God and thereby guarantees that married couples lead a holy and God-fearing life.

Cooperating in the Sin of One's Spouse

It may happen that one spouse may want to use the marital act in an illicit manner. He or she may want to resort to artificial birth control methods or

[37] FC 32.

withdrawal, or even indulge in deviant sex. What must the other spouse do in this case? Must one refuse or give in? The latter option is what we mean by cooperating in the sin of one's spouse. One's cooperation may be "formal," whereby one either openly or secretly approves of the other's behavior. On the other hand, "material" or "passive" cooperation consists in external or internal disapproval of the sin of the other.

Formal cooperation is always sinful because one participates in and approves of a sinful act. Passive or material cooperation, on the other hand, may be licit under certain circumstances, as when the innocent spouse is forced to give in even if he or she forthrightly objects to engaging in an illicit act. Material cooperation however becomes illicit when the innocent spouse provokes the sinful act in a direct way by stating, for instance, that he or she no longer wants to have more children, or in an indirect way, like complaining about the discomforts of having a new baby.

The innocent spouse, however, may be a passive accomplice of the other and *not* commit a sin, in the following situations:

- *coitus interruptus*, or withdrawal on the part of the husband;
- when the other spouse has undergone permanent or temporary sterilization, surgically or by taking non-abortifacient medicines, or when the husband insists on using contraceptive devices while engaging in sexual intercourse;
- in cases of sodomy, the innocent spouse who resists either openly or inwardly, is never an accomplice.

We must however clarify that passive cooperation is licit only if it is called for to avoid more serious problems in the household, like grave family discord, or a serious threat of sexual incontinence or the risk of adultery if the other spouse would not give in.

When the said risks are immediate and especially at hand, the innocent spouse may even licitly ask for the marital debt, even if one very well knows that the other spouse would abuse it. Nevertheless, the above-mentioned reasons will never make cooperation in abortion licit. When a woman takes an abortifacient treatment, her husband becomes an accomplice not just in a sinful sexual act, but also in a possible abortion—an abomination that surpasses all the evil and harm that one probably would want to avoid by passively cooperating in the sinful behavior of one's spouse.

The Pedagogy of Chastity

As teacher and mother, the Church never tires of proclaiming the moral norm that must guide the trans-mission of life. She is in no way the author or the arbiter of this norm. Faithful to Jesus Christ, she interprets the moral norms and teaches it without concealing its demands. As Mother, the Church stands by those married couples who find themselves in difficult situation; she is aware of their struggle and understands their uncertainties. As Mother, she does not want the truth falsified or watered down just to resolve conjugal problems. She knows that there can be no contradiction between the divine law as regards the responsible transmission of life and the fostering of authentic married love.

To know the divine designs on human love one needs clear, timely, and serious instruction and education that fosters self-mastery and discipline. This shows the need to cultivate the virtue of chastity, which does not signify a rejection of human sexuality or the lack of esteem for it. Rather, it represents spiritual energy that is capable of defending one's love from the perils of selfishness and aggression and which can develop human love to its fullest meaning. The practice of chastity is a positive effort, an affirmation of love. It neither curtails affection nor diminishes its human qualities, but rather elevates it to the divine. The moral norms serve as a guide for spouses so that they may gradually learn to apply them to concrete cases. Chastity is not an unattainable ideal but a divine command; and in order to live it, God gives us his grace.

The pedagogy of chastity, therefore, cannot be isolated from the overall content of married life, the framework within which husband and wife are called to be holy. Sacrifice cannot be removed from family life if the love of the spouses is deepened and becomes a source of intimate joy. There are many married couples who, due to serious reasons, agree to practice periodic continence and thereby acquire a greater sense of responsibility and maturity in their attitude towards life and love. Their human joy and peace of soul are fruit of fulfilling God's will. This should be the best incentive for those who still harbor doubts about the matter. It is a difficult but undoubtedly worthwhile endeavor. It demands sacrifice but also makes one a better person. It requires struggle but it also endows the conjugal union with human and spiritual blessings.

The consequences are serenity and peace of mind in facing and resolving all sorts of problems. One then learns to overcome selfishness, the enemy of true love; one gains moral authority and, with it, the capacity to educate one's children in a deep, effective and more lasting way. The moral norms were never meant to give anyone a hard time; they rather constitute the path to marital happiness. Moreover, divine grace is never lacking, especially if the spouses have recourse to prayer and the sacraments of Penance and the Holy Eucharist.

This is a battle for winners because its goal is to love God and to go deeper in one's love for the other.

7

The Sacrament of Matrimony

"The matrimonial covenant, by which a man and a woman establish between themselves a partnership of the whole of life, is by its nature ordered toward the good of the spouses and the procreation and education of offspring; this covenant between baptized persons has been raised by Christ the Lord to the dignity of a sacrament." [1]

The divine value of Matrimony is rooted in its being a sacrament, one of the seven sacred signs instituted by Christ to give grace and to advance the sanctification of those he redeemed. This idea cannot be taken for granted. Married couples should pause and ponder that God created a specific sacrament for them so that they may overcome all the obstacles that come their way and so that they may enjoy all the blessings of married life in an atmosphere blessed by the warmth of God's love and grace.

[1] *CCC* 1601.

Catholic marriages bear the indissoluble mark of the love Christ has as Bridegroom of the Church. Matrimony then is an effective sign, a sacrament, of Christ's union with his Church, whom he has taken as his wife. This is how the apostle Paul explains this mystical link: *Husbands, love your wives as Christ loved the church and gave himself up for her, that he might sanctify her.*[2]

As he was about to begin his public life, Jesus performed his first miracle, at his Mother's request, during a wedding feast. The Church has always conferred great significance to the Lord's actions here: His presence sanctified that wedding. The Church therefore sees that the Lord not only confirms the goodness of the conjugal union but also proclaims that, from then on, Christian marriage will always be an effective sign of Christ's presence in the married couple. It is a presence that bestows light and strength for the spouses to carry out their common project—as a couple and as a family. The grace obtained from the sacrament of marriage is divine, a precious fruit of the Cross which is the source of all Christian life. God is the author of the conjugal union and he has made the commitment to be forever present in it, the way that he established a Covenant with all of mankind, the way Christ is espoused to the Church.

This is why Max Thurian wrote that marriage is not simply a contract entered into by a man and a woman who agree to be faithful to each other. God personally makes this mysterious union possible and protects it against all dangers. This is the primordial characteristic of a Christian marriage: It is a union

[2] Eph 5: 25-26.

made by God and in God.[3] Sacred Scriptures then make much sense: *What therefore God has joined together, let no man put asunder.*[4] And it makes even more sense when one sees it from the logical perspective that it is God who unites all married couples. They express their gift of self by means of a personal and irrevocable exchange of consent that establishes the marital bond and which brings with it the seal and guarantee of total and definitive mutual self-giving.

Marriage is a sacred reality in itself. Its sacramental nature is not an "add-on" or an accent piece, somewhat like what jewelry or the right bag or shoes do to pull together an outfit. It is a reality that belongs to Matrimony's very essence. It gives a special stamp to the union of the baptized man and woman, marking it with the seal of Christ. All sacraments have a direct connection with the Paschal mystery: their strength and effectiveness are rooted in the Passion, Death and Resurrection of Christ as expressed in the mystery of the Eucharist. This is why marriages are celebrated during Holy Mass. In the Mass, one celebrates the memorial of the New Covenant that Jesus established with his Church.

The exchange of vows between husband and wife is modeled after Christ's marriage with his beloved spouse for whom he died and with whom he is united for always. Similarly, spouses offer their entire lives to each other, in union with the Lord's offering to his Church as manifested in the sacrifice of the Eucharist. When the spouses receive the Body and Blood of Christ

[3] Cf. M. Thurian, *Mariage et celibat. Dons et appels*, Taizé, 1977, 27-28.
[4] Mt 19:6.

in Holy Communion, the two become one body with Christ as well. This should explain our earlier statement, that in every marriage the couple stands at the altar with God between them.

Christ elevated Matrimony to the order of grace. From then on, every union between two baptized people takes on a sacramental nature. Two Catholics cannot contract marriage without contracting the sacrament at the same time. For as long as they live, their union remains a mysterious symbol of Christ's grace. But there is more. It is the contracting parties who administer the sacrament to each other. Although Christ is the sole and principal Minister of all the sacraments, in marriage, the spouses are God's instruments to impart the gratuitous graces and supernatural blessings of marriage to one other. In so doing the spouses in a way participate in Christ's priesthood which they received at Baptism, the sacrament that made them living members of the People of God.

It is Christ who goes out of his way to seek out the husband and the wife in their exercise of mutual self-giving. It is Christ who offers them the strength they need to compensate for their weaknesses and to bolster their fragile sense of freedom, the very freedom that brought them to say with all sincerity, "I take you as my husband (wife)…till death do us part." They utter these words with hands outstretched, signifying that they are ready to face the risks and challenges that this world has in store for them and which can nullify these noble words and gestures on grounds of "freedom," "choice," and "basic human rights."

In the prayers of the liturgy of the sacrament of Matrimony, the spouses invoke the Holy Spirit to come upon them so that their union may be transformed into Christ's communion of love with the Church. The Holy Spirit seals this covenant. He is the ever-abundant source of love, and the strength to renew their faithfulness to each other. He consecrates their duties to each other and the dignity of their new status as married persons. Conjugal love, so to speak, is assumed into the Divine Love. Through this grace, the couple perfects their love and strengthens their union so that they can effectively help each other struggle to be holy in their married life and to properly bring up their children who are the fruit of their mutual self-giving. It is Christ himself who seeks them out. And he abides, granting them the strength to follow him up the path to Calvary. He is there to lift them from their falls and to help them forgive each other and to bear each other's burden with patience and understanding.

Tertulian wrote centuries ago: "From where do I draw strength to best describe the blessedness of matrimony that the Church celebrates, to confirm the offering, to seal the blessings? The angels proclaim it, the heavenly Father ratifies it…What marriage there is for two Christians, united by a single hope, a single desire, a single discipline, a single service! Nothing, neither spirit nor the flesh, shall ever separate the two, children of the same Father, servants of the same Lord. Rather they are truly two who have become one. For where there is the union of flesh, there is also the union of the spirit."

When the Son of God became man, he wanted to give his disciples everything they needed to be as perfect as his heavenly Father is perfect. When Christ endowed Matrimony with great transcendence, he clearly states that he is not giving his followers a simple social institution but something infinitely greater. Christ was not out to fix messy social structures; His mission was to institute and to provide us the human means to reach Heaven. And Matrimony is one of these means.

St Paul gave the Ephesians a very real and concrete illustration of this, in the context of Christ's indissoluble union with his Mystical Body.[5] This mystery cannot be belittled or downplayed, which is why everything that has to do with the marital relationship ought to be approached and expressed in a way similar to Jesus' love for his Church, the way the Head cares for his entire Body. Both spouses therefore hold the great and grand responsibility to do everything possible to remain true to the grace given to them. They cannot make a sham of the model God himself has fashioned for them.

The sacramental nature of their union should deeply impress on the couples' minds the new manner in which they have been assimilated into Jesus Christ.

---

[5] *Be subject to one another out of reverence for Christ. Wives, be subject to your husbands, as to the Lord. For the husband is the head of the wife as Christ is the head of the church, his body, and is himself its Savior. ... Husbands, love your wives, as Christ loved the church and gave himself up for her, that he might sanctify her... Even so husbands should love their wives as their own bodies. He who loves his wife loves himself. For no man ever hates his own flesh, but nourishes and cherishes it, as Christ does the church, because we are members of his body. For his reason a man shall leave his father and mother and be joined to his wife, and the two shall become one. This is a great mystery, and I mean in reference to Christ and the church.* (Eph 5:21-32).

Their mission is to transform their marriage into a living and permanent testimony of the bond that unites Christ with his Church. By virtue of this supernatural consecration, spouses are given a special role to play in the life of the Church. They are called to collaborate with God in the growth of the Mystical Body of Christ; their principal mission is to be the primary educators of their offspring, forming them in the image of the Son of God. "When Christian spouses get married, it is not only their own adventure which they embark upon— even though we understand this adventure in terms of sanctification and mission; they embark upon an adventure of the universal history of salvation."[6]

With this end in view, the sacrament of Matrimony confers on them the grace and the duty to live up to their responsibilities before God and to give good example to their children. The sacrament helps them fulfill the obligations of love that they have towards each other and towards their children; it makes them more understanding, forgiving, considerate, and helpful, and leads them to renew their love when the moment calls for it.

"Conjugal love involves a totality, in which all the elements of the person enter—appeal of the body and instinct, power of feeling and affectivity, aspiration of the spirit and of the will. It aims at a deeply personal unity, the unity that, beyond union in one flesh, leads to forming one heart and soul; it demands *indissolubility* and *faithfulness* in definitive mutual giving; and it is open to *fertility* (cf. *Humanae vitae*) In a word, it is a

[6] John Paul II, *Address to the Youth in the Basilica of St Peter*, 3 January 1979; *Homily at Nowy Targ*, Poland, 8 June 1979.

question of the normal characteristics of all natural conjugal love, but with a new significance which not only purifies and strengthens them, but raises them to the extent of making them the expression of specifically Christian values."[7]

Jesus Christ constantly accompanies the spouses as they carry out their mission. Indeed, these words apply to them: *Again I say to you, if two of you agree on earth about anything they ask, it will be done for them by my Father in heaven. For where two or three are gathered in my name, there am I in the midst of them.*[8] Sin alone obstructs the full exercise of a Christian's configuration to Christ. Sin may not destroy this completely but it deprives one of the light and splendor that comes from being close to God.

We can further appreciate the sacramental nature of Matrimony as a marvelous reality in one's married life with the following considerations.

The spouses may not be constantly conscious of it, but their reciprocal love is deeply inspired by God's love. Their love comes from him and so to him it should return. Every manifestation of love and respect, every sacrifice and sorrow, whatever they may find sweet and whatever may require patience, every moment of rest and work—in a word, every second in family life is infused with the divine. God is present in every family event, from the most important to the most commonplace, and it is there that spouses should try to find him. Christ seals and perfects every intimate moment and every gesture of affection. Again, the spouses may not be completely aware of it, but their mutual love is

[7] *FC* 13.
[8] Mt 18:19-20.

Christ's Love. Their love for each other is Christ's love for his Church and an echo of the intimate Love of the Blessed Trinity: Love moved the Father to send his Son into the world, and it is the Love between the Father and the Son that brings forth (or, in theological terms, "spirates") the Holy Spirit.

"What riches, what exigencies, what dynamism spring forth, if this sacrament is lived from day to day, in faith, in the image of the reciprocal gift of Christ and his Church! What strength when spouses have the simplicity to help each other, under the eyes of the Lord, to progress in their faith, in their mutual love, if need be in their forgiveness, in their common commitment to serve their family, the Church community, and the social milieu!"[9]

The duty of the spouses to be holy proceeds from this very idea. God has singled them out to make their conjugal and family relationships divine. Christians are called to sanctity in their own homes, amidst the day-to-day realities of family life. What's more, the sacrament of Matrimony confers a special grace to make them apt for the job and to turn their home into an authentic center for Christian virtues.

Another point to consider is that conjugal spirituality is fully lay and secular in nature. This means that married couples seek to be holy in the fulfillment of their ordinary duties, which is in no way related to the spirituality of the religious orders. The channel through which sanctifying grace—the Holy Spirit's action on souls—reaches the spouses befits the specific sacramental character that they have received. To be

[9] John Paul II, *Address to the International Council of the Movement Equipes Notre Dame*, September 17, 1979.

holy, all that the couple have to do is to follow with love and fidelity the road that they have taken, counting on the help of sacramental grace all through their lives, and to inculcate in their children the teachings of Christ and the virtues extolled in the Gospels.

"In this manner, they offer all men the example of unwearying and generous love; in this way they build up the brotherhood of charity; in so doing they stand as the witnesses and cooperators in the fruitfulness of Holy Mother Church; by such lives, they are a sign and a participation in that very love, with which Christ loved his Bride and for which he delivered himself up for her."[10]

Christian marriage is a divine path on Earth, a way of sanctification and a seedbed of salvation. In it and, more importantly, through it, the spouses find all that they need to direct their lives and that of their offspring towards God. In it, they fulfill their supernatural vocation. Divine Revelation tells us that married life is a symbol of Christ's love for the Church[11] and a practical manifestation of its likeness to God[12] in the sense that when husband and wife, parents and children show their human and supernatural love for each other, they experience a personal encounter with Jesus Christ. *And the King will answer them, 'Truly I say to you, as you did it to one of the least of these my brethren, you did it to me.'*[13]

Holiness which is the fruit of knowing that one's marriage is blessed with sacramental grace is one that

---

[10] *LG* 41.
[11] Cf. Eph 5:25.
[12] *God is love* (1 Jn 6:3).
[13] Mt 25:40.

is replete with spontaneity and simplicity. For the baptized Christian, one's ordinary life can surely be holy and God-centered. The Lord calls them to make their daily experiences divine, that is to give divine dignity to their daily tasks, to live a fully Christian life amidst the daily grind, and to do things with love and out of love. The house of Nazareth precisely breathes of this atmosphere, and we can contemplate its finer details in the life of the Blessed Virgin Mary.

"We can't forget that Mary spent nearly every day of her life just like millions of other women who look after their family, bring up their children and take care of the house. Mary sanctifies the ordinary everyday things—what some people wrongly regard as unimportant and insignificant: everyday work, looking after those closest to you, visits to friends and relatives. What a blessed ordinariness that can be so full of love of God! For that's what explains Mary's life—her love. A complete love, so complete that she forgets herself and is happy just to be there where God wants her, fulfilling with care what God wants her to do. That is why even her slightest action is never routine or vain but, rather, full of meaning. Mary, our mother, is for us both an example and a way. We have to try to be like her, in the ordinary circumstances in which God wants us to live."[14]

The Second Vatican Council solemnly highlights the sanctifying reality of conjugal love by explaining that it is precisely the same way that God took in times past when he sought to establish a Covenant with the Chosen People. The nature of this covenant was one of

[14] *Christ is Passing By* no. 148.

love and faithfulness, much like that of a marriage bond. Likewise, in the New Covenant, God entered into a spousal relationship with his people when he revealed himself as the Bridegroom of his Church. In this light, God engages in an encounter with Christian spouses through the sacrament of Matrimony. And he abides with them so that, just as he loves his Church and died for her, spouses ought to love and give themselves to each other totally, perpetually and faithfully. This self giving seems all too human, but it has a supernatural dimension to it: Conjugal love is assumed into Divine Love. Thanks to Christ's redemptive work and the saving action of the Church, the love of husband and wife is firmly incorporated and endowed with infinite wealth, with God personally guiding the spouses to himself. And they can count on this superior—omnipotent—assistance as they fulfill their roles as husband and wife as well as when they carry out their sublime mission as father and mother.

Marriage as a sacrament consecrates (that is, makes sacred) the dignity of the married status and the consequent family duties. If the spouses follow the way of Christ in fulfilling their responsibilities to each other and to their children, then their life shall always be permeated with faith, hope and charity. They make daily progress toward being better persons and support each other on the road to heaven.[15] This is the "new covenant" that they established on their wedding day. The sacrament that they received gives them enduring strength to be virtuous and to strive every day to be a better spouse and a better parent. This is the manner

[15] Cf. *GS* 48.

with which married couples give glory to God. Thus, for those who get married with a true sense of vocation, their union—their entire life—takes on a divine face even while they are here on Earth; and for a Christian, this dimension should assimilate all the rest.

"The sacrament of matrimony is not simply a religious ceremony that sanctifies a human act. It is the seed planted in the soul that yields fruit all throughout one's married life. In a sense, it inspires all the actions and sentiments of the married couple and urges them to give supernatural meaning to their life. It predisposes them to the ideals of sanctity that God personally planted in their souls on their wedding day."[16]

The spouses then embark on a special journey with God as their traveling companion. He supports them and participates in their love. He invites them to a divine level of existence which they must undertake together, where one always lives for the other. The spouses therefore bind themselves to a common duty of seeking the love of God together, discovering him in each other, and to aspire to live a full Christian life precisely in their new life as a couple. In this case, all the ordinary things that they live and touch take on a divine meaning and lead them to holiness.

[16] J. Leclerq, *Christian Marriage,* 146.

8

The Sanctification of Matrimony

SANCTITY AND THE WILL OF GOD

"Marriage is not only a refuge of love and human happiness. It is most especially a genuine setting for the sanctification of those who believe in Christ the Lord. Married couples are called to a personal encounter with God in the vicissitudes of ordinary life; to participate in a very effective way in forming the new children of the Church in the faith; and to extend the beneficial influence of the home to the rest of the community and to the other members of the People of God."[1]

The mission of Christian spouses and of the families they form is of great importance to the life of the Church. Anyone who wishes to see the home as the setting for one's sanctification will bear in mind this first idea: that one's existence has a vocational meaning. The spirituality of married couples is based

[1] Gonzalo Lobo, *Person, Family, Society* Madrid, 1973, 139.

on the undeniable fact that they have been called to carry out a well-defined mission in very specific circumstances. And it is only by carrying out this mission that they can please God.

Spiritual life, or the struggle to be holy, is not a question of counting the number of prayers said every day or of undergoing great trials and sufferings. To be a saint means more than performing difficult or troublesome tasks for God. Many people think that holiness is not their way because they do not pray as piously as others or are unable to do great sacrifices. There is no doubt that prayer and sacrifice are essential to living an authentic Christian life, but we also must remember Jesus' words. *Not every one who says to me, 'Lord, Lord,' shall enter the kingdom of heaven, but he who does the will of my Father who is in heaven.*[2]

But then, what is his will? How can we recognize it?" How can we be sure that we are doing God's will and not our own? There is a way: Be a soul of prayer. Live in the state of grace. Be docile to the voice of the Holy Spirit in your soul. "First of all, docility because it is the Holy Spirit who, with his inspirations, gives a supernatural tone to our thoughts, desires, and actions. It is he who leads us to receive Christ's teaching and to assimilate it in a profound way. It is he who gives us the light by which we perceive our personal calling and the strength to carry out all that God expects of us."[3]

Without prayer, without a personal friendship with Jesus Christ, without a deep and sincere examination of conscience, without spiritual guidance, it will be

[2] Mt 7:21.
[3] *Christ is Passing By* no. 135.

impossible to follow God's will because we will never be able to recognize it. Moreover, we risk taking the wrong path, and most probably the more comfortable one which will lead us away from our real goal. This is what St Augustine meant when he exclaimed, "You are running well, but off-track!" We need to ask the Lord frequently, in a sincere and personal dialogue, "Lord, what do you want of me now? What do you want me to do in this situation?" This is the only way to discover what we should do at every moment.

"Holy Spirit, Love of the Father and the Son: inspire me always to think what I ought, to say what I should and how to say it, to keep silence when I should and what I must put to writing. And to pray as I should. What I must do for your greater glory, the good of souls and my own sanctification." (Cardinal Vedrier)

To understand the importance of discovering and doing God's will, let us reflect on some lessons from the Gospel that illustrate the value of fulfilling a command to the last detail. Through these parables, the Lord makes it clear that fidelity counts most where small things are concerned. He speaks of some virgins who were supposed to accompany the bride and the bridegroom to the marriage feast. However the bridegroom was delayed and the virgins grew tired of waiting and fell asleep. The oil of their lamps was consumed and the light died out. Some of the virgins had foresight and brought extra oil to fill their lamps. They were ready once more to meet the bridegroom. The other virgins however had to leave to buy more oil. When the bridegroom finally showed up, he welcomed the virgins who had their lamps lit and shut the door.

When the other virgins returned, they knocked long and hard on the door for the bridegroom to let them in. But they did so in vain. They had lost their chance. They wanted to attend to the newlyweds but could not because they neglected a small detail: the oil. They ran and shouted, *'Lord, Lord, open to us!' But he replied, 'Truly, I say to you, I do not know you.'*[4]

Jesus repeats this lesson in many other ways: when He sought fruit from the barren fig tree and was disappointed to find none; in the parable about the lazy servant who did not use his one talent to yield the profit expected by his master; the parable of the steward who squandered the goods entrusted to him; and the parable of the vigilant householder who made sure that thieves could not break into his house.[5]

When Jesus describes the Last Judgment, he says that reward awaits those who, without waiting for a special sign from heaven or without hardly realizing it at all, generously and faithfully fulfill the mission entrusted to them. In the Last Judgment, after each man has rendered an account of his life, God shall reward the righteous. *For I was hungry and you gave me food, I was thirsty and you gave me drink, I was a stranger and you welcomed me, I was naked and you clothed me, I was sick and you visited me, I was in prison and you came to me. Then the righteous will answer him, 'Lord, when did we see thee hungry and feed thee, or thirsty and give thee drink? And when did we see thee a stranger and welcome thee, or naked and clothe thee? And when did we see thee sick or in prison and visit thee?' And the King will answer*

---

[4] Mt 25:1-13.
[5] Cf. Mt 21:18-22; Mt 25:14-30; Mt 24:45-51; Mt 24:42-44.

them, 'Truly I say to you, as you did it to one of the least of these my brethren, you did it to me. [6]

Then again, there are others who will be taken by surprise. These are the people who failed in their mission, or wasted their time, or omitted a good act that they were perfectly capable of doing. Punishment therefore inescapably awaits them and the Holy Spirit tells us why in another part of Sacred Scripture. *Whoever knows what is right to do and fails to do it, for him it is sin.* [7] Those who were condemned were punished on account of their irresponsibility. They committed a sin of omission. They neglected to do what God expected of them. This parable gives married couples and parents much to think about. They can draw many lessons from it and formulate specific resolutions to improve their family life. Since they are called to sanctify themselves in the home, they ought to conscientiously fulfill the big as well as the small obligations of married life.

We have seen how fidelity to one's spouse is made up of small duties:

• No one else should occupy one's heart and life other than one's spouse;

• Spouses ought to give each other warmth and affection so that their love would not grow cold;

• They must work at understanding and respecting each other;

• They must get to know each other so deeply that they immediately know what would make the other happy;

[6] Mt 25:35-40.
[7] Jas 4:17.

• They must attend to each other's smallest needs and concerns.

Many little things are easily overlooked because one forgets or takes them for granted. Yet remember that to deny one's spouse or child any token of love, no matter how small, is to deny Christ himself. One cannot underestimate the value of the little details because these spell the difference between success and failure in a marriage. Only the person who cares for the little things in daily life will hear at one's deathbed these words of Christ, *Well done, good and faithful servant; you have been faithful over a little, I will set you over much; enter into the joy of your master.*[8]

Such omissions can also damage the parent-child relationship. This happens when parents take no serious interest in knowing their children well, that is, their temperament, their virtues and talents, and their defects and limitations. Some parents, out of timidity, laziness or cowardice, neglect their children's education. They do not bother knowing the kind of books or magazines they read, the friends they hang around with, or the movies or shows they watch. They have no clue about how their children are performing in school. Neither do they exert effort to discipline them or teach them self-mastery. They do not speak to them, in clear and prudent terms, about the nature of sex and the mystery of human life but leave the job to ignorant, shady or malicious sources. Then there are parents who do not try to treat the children fairly and show favoritism, oblivious that every child is unique and must be appreciated for what he or she is.

[8] Mt 25:21.

Surely, this long list of oversights is not always due to bad will. Mom is caught up with the household chores, or ironically organizing social projects like a lecture on "how to raise your children right." Dad has "urgent stuff" at work. He invokes his "inviolable right" to unwind when he comes home from work and leaves the "educating" to his wife. Sad to say, many husbands believe that their sole duty is to earn enough money to get the wife and kids a new house and a fancy car. Still, one can give a million and one lame excuses. One therefore cannot be surprised to see his family life far from ideal—if not almost dysfunctional—if he neglects the proper upbringing of the children. And neither can he expect God to judge him kindly when he stands before the Judgment Seat.

THE CONSTANT PRACTICE OF CHRISTIAN VIRTUES

The foundation of Christian life consists in adhering to God's will, living constantly in the state of grace, and faithfully corresponding to the actual graces bestowed by God on the soul. Grace is given by God for one to nurture and cultivate so that it may yield abundant fruit. Thus one must first be willing to continuously exert the effort to make grace yield fruits of sanctity and love. A person must strive to practice the different virtues that define a Christian because it is these virtues that characterize one's daily living and dealings. The relationship between husband and wife, parents and children, as well as one's dealings with the household help, friends and co-workers are all occasions to live the virtues that lead one to sanctity.

Spouses mature and improve by the day as they tirelessly work at acquiring and deepening good habits. And if their effort is God-centered, their trust in the help of grace and the desire to please him will make them more cheerful, and optimistic. A vibrant supernatural life not only makes one progress along the road to holiness; it is also the secret of perpetual youthfulness.

However, as we have said, supernatural life is not just made up of a string of prayers. Rather, it is a general attitude of seeing God's hand in the ordinary events of the day. It is an attitude of having one's gaze constantly fixed on the Lord in whom *we live and move and have our being*.[9] This makes us see God as a good and very approachable Father. It brings us to dare call him "Daddy."

"It's necessary to be convinced that God is always near us. Too often we live as though our Lord were somewhere far off—where the stars shine. We fail to realize that he is also by our side—always.

For he is a loving Father. He loves each one of us more than all the mothers in the world can love their children, helping us and inspiring us, blessing...and forgiving.

How often we've erased the frowns from our parents' brows, telling them after some prank, 'I won't do it again!' Maybe that same day we fall again...And our father, with feigned harshness in his voice and a serious face, reproves us, while at the same time his heart is softened because he knows our weakness: 'Poor boy,' thinks, 'How hard he tries to behave well.'

[9] Acts 17:28.

We have to be completely convinced, realizing it to the full, that our Lord, who is close to us and in heaven, is a Father, and very much *our* Father."[10]

The similarity between our awareness that we are children both of our earthly parents and of our Father God is a clue to understanding why practicing the virtues in the home has divine overtones. Nothing accomplished on Earth with the intention of carrying out God's will is of ephemeral value. The very same virtues that must be cultivated at home by parents and children alike must also be lived by every Christian who wishes to sanctify his ordinary life. First of these virtues are the supernatural ones—faith, hope and charity—which God infuses into the soul with grace. There are also the human or the natural virtues, which belong to a different order but are closely linked with the supernatural and therefore deeply influence the spiritual life. The interplay of the human and the supernatural virtues marks the road that married couples must follow if their life together should lead them to heaven.

Faith

Faith is the foundation of all the virtues. Without faith, it is impossible to please God.[11] The entire life of grace flows from faith.[12] Faith implies a deep awareness of God's fatherly concern for His children and leads us to say with St Paul *We know that in everything God*

---

[10] *The Way* no. 267.
[11] Cf. Heb 10:5-10.
[12] Cf. Rom 5:1.

works for good with those who love him.[13] This is why a person with faith knows how to face daily events— good or bad—with a supernatural attitude. A man of faith knows how to use these events to gratefully unite himself with the Lord. Faith makes him serenely face big or small trials because he knows that God only wants what is good for us. Moreover, the man of faith knows that God never deprives us of his grace as long as we do all we can, humanly speaking, and at the same time beg him to fill in for that which is already beyond our strength and resources. A person who lives by faith is characterized by constant optimism and good humor in the face of annoyances and difficulties. A man of faith judges events and things with the eyes of God, never losing sight of their repercussions unto eternity.

On the other hand, a person without faith feels defeated at the first skirmish. Any problem, large or small, is enough to make him throw in the towel. Even on the human plane, a home is plunged into chaos when spouses lose faith in each other or when parents mistrust their children and become pessimistic about the effectiveness of the advice and good example that they give. A Christian who loses faith in God and His fatherly protection suffers uselessly; he abandons the spiritual struggle and falls into despair.

Hope

Married life should be filled with great ambitions to love and to be happy. It is simply un-Christian for

[13] Rom 8:28.

spouses to take on fatalistic attitude towards events and just watch the years pass them by. A Christian couple launch themselves into marriage convinced that Christ awaits them at the end of the road. Therefore, they must persevere everyday in their effort to renew their love for each other. Of course, they will have their share of problems and setbacks, mistakes and petty quarrels—even major tragedies. In all this they must try to firmly nurture the theological virtue of hope in their hearts. They must have that supernatural certainty that any event can be turned to their benefit because as they strive to overcome daily trials, they advance along the road to holiness.

Married couples who live this way can be assured that God fulfills all his promises to those who believe in him: *May the God of hope fill you with all joy and peace in believing, so that by the power of the Holy Spirit you may abound in hope.*[14] They must never forsake their yearning for sanctity and be determined to persevere till the end, seconding at all times the prompting of grace. The Holy Spirit assures us that God finishes off every work of sanctification that he has started[15] on the condition, however, that the soul strives to correct its mistakes, overcome its defects, and remain cheerful and serene. Faithful until death: this is how one must live, not giving in to weariness or discouragement. These supernatural considerations should likewise apply to the more human facets of family life. Sacramental grace affords the means to win the big and small battles of the day. Nothing is ever hopelessly

[14] Rom 15:13.
[15] *And I am sure that he who began a good work in you will bring it to completion at the day of Jesus Christ.* (Phil 1:6).

lost. There is a solution to everything, provided we do not lose heart. The important thing is to keep one's head, trust in God and use the means he has given to put up a steadfast fight.

No doubt, certain situations may call for heroism. But even in these cases, a Christian is no pessimist; he does not exaggerate the negative side of things. A pessimist is already beaten even before he jumps into the fray. A loser can say, "We'll never make it." He may be right, from a certain perspective. A winner, however, can say "Maybe not, but we can try and gain some ground." It is all a question of attitude.

One must be optimistic, not because optimism guarantees success, but because it makes one work more cheerfully and spare himself needless anguish. This is why doctors try to lift their patients' spirits. They know that medicine can do little for terminally-ill patients who have lost the will to live; but for a patient who cheerfully pushes on, the medicine simply helps speed up the recovery. Similarly, in a family, hope undeniably begets optimism, and optimism in turn breeds the fighting spirit married couples need to win their war against selfishness and unhinged passion. God will never deny them his help if they struggle. They must remember St Paul's experience of being weighed down by the persistent "sting" of his weaknesses. He asked the Lord to free him of it, but the Lord gave him a clear reply: *My grace is sufficient for you, for my power is made perfect in weakness.*[16]

---

[16] 2 Cor 12:9.

Charity

Charity is the most important virtue for a Christian. It gives meaning to what he does and direction to his dealings with God and neighbor. It is not enough to have faith or to be long-suffering or magnanimous to the poor: For *if I have prophetic powers, and understand all mysteries and all knowledge, and if I have all faith, so as to remove mountains, but have not love, I am nothing. If I give away all I have, and if I deliver my body to be burned, but have not love, I gain nothing.*[17]

We have spoken at length about the love of married couples and of its relationship with the love of God. Married life is built on love and should be adorned with the virtues that spring from love. Hence, all that St Paul says about charity can truly be applied to life in the home: *Love is patient and kind; love is not jealous or boastful; it is not arrogant or rude. Love does not insist on its own way; it is not irritable or resentful; it does not rejoice at wrong, but rejoices in the right. Love bears all things, believes all things, hopes all things, endures all things.*[18]

Charity therefore should not be understood as coldly tolerating the character or opinion of another. It is rather genuine warmth, affection and kindness. It finds expression in apparently trivial things, like keeping the home spick and span; preparing warm and tasty meals; smiling despite a bad mood; respecting each one's legitimate privacy; being amiable to others; being considerate of the others' opinions, preferences, and even the smallest whims and wishes; keeping

[17] 1 Cor 13:2-3.
[18] 1 Cor 13:4-7.

quiet when others need to sleep or study. Within the overall scheme of charity, such "trifles" do mean so much.

The Moral Virtues

We are not going to rattle off an exhaustive list. We only wish to stress how everything that improves a person as a human being and as a Christian has positive impact on family life because, through the practice of the virtues, a person becomes mature and therefore helps bring peace to the home.

Prudence

A prudent wife knows how to hold her tongue when she sees that some legitimate question, complaint or reproach can be saved for a better moment. She holds her peace when she sees her husband engrossed in work problems or is simply exhausted. Likewise, a prudent husband refrains from making too many demands on his wife if he sees her in no condition to taken on strenuous household work or to engage in the marital act. Prudent parents plan the upbringing of their children, striking a balance between discipline and affection. Prudence is a far cry from cowardice or rashness. It leads one to discern matters, establish correct goals, and to formulate a plan of action with foresight, initiative, courage and sound judgment.

Fortitude

One needs this virtue to stand tall in the face of problems and to avoid conflicts. Fortitude keeps one unflustered in the face of the unforeseen. It helps one to avoid complaining when unpleasant things such as sickness or temporary setbacks arise.

Temperance

This virtue is needed to acquire self-mastery in speech, as well as to check the inclination to seek pleasure in a disorderly and degrading way. One needs temperance to live total self-surrender in marital life.

Justice

Justice makes a person constantly disposed to respect the right of one's family to be loved. It leads one to faithfully fulfill his obligations and to respect the dignity of all, from the youngest child, to the domestic staff, to one's neighbors and other people whom one gets in touch with in one way or the other.

Obedience

This most important virtue is one that is all too often scorned nowadays. Obedience is not a servile loss of one's personality. It is the free surrender of self to the will of God, and the readiness to comply with the reasonable requests of another. St Paul, in one famous passage, exhorts wives to obey their husbands the way the Church submits herself to Christ, her Head, and for husbands to love their wives the way God loves his Church and died for her. *Be subject to one another out of reverence for Christ. Wives, be subject to your husbands, as to the Lord. For the husband is the head of the wife as Christ is the head of the church, his body, and is himself its Savior. As the church is subject to Christ, so let wives also be subject in everything to their husbands. Husbands, love your wives as Christ loved the church and gave himself up for her, that he might sanctify her...*[19] Obedience also means abiding by the laws of the Church and State. It means fulfilling all civic and religious duties, from the simplest traffic regulation to the most solemn expressions of the divine will as laid down in the Ten Commandments.

Humility

Humility is closely related to obedience, much like a tree's roots are to its fruits. It is impossible for a proud person to be obedient. Husband and wife need to be humble if they want to have a happy home. A humble person avoids breeding personal problems but instead gives himself to other unstintingly, without expecting anything in return. He serves others without expecting to be thanked. Humility makes it easier to form and raise a family. It is reflected in the effort to hide one's tiredness and, instead of being fussy, bossy or overbearing, one tries to be gentle and approachable and to serve without show. Humility is a great means to be holy and happy, and to make others happy.

[19] Eph 5:21-26.

Simplicity

A simple person tempers one's words and angry reactions. He says things in a positive way and never thinks that he is always right. He knows how to apologize and make amends. He does not take himself too seriously and always esteems the good points of other people. Simplicity is an essential characteristic of a truly Christian family.[20]

Spirit of detachment and poverty

Obviously, this does not mean depriving one's self of material possessions. "If riches abound, set not your heart upon them. Strive rather, to use them generously —and if necessary, heroically. Be poor of spirit."[21] When one is poor in spirit, one's heart is not tied down by any material possession or intellectual pursuit. One does not seek personal advancement to the detriment of the higher values of love of God and neighbor. A father and a mother live poverty when they give each thing its due importance. They do not get hysterical when something gets lost or broken. They take the bus, the subway or even walk with as much ease as when they can use the family car. They generously share their material prosperity, no matter how little or great this may be, in the interest of their family and for the good of those in need.

Every Christian has to learn to be poor in spirit. Many do not find this easy because they immediately picture poverty as a life of misery and filth, or, at best,

[20] Cf. *Conversations...* no. 108.
[21] *The Way* no. 636.

one of admirable austerity, typical of a convent or monastery. However, a better grasp of this virtue leads one to realize that Christian poverty is not simply a renunciation of material possessions, even though it does entail doing away with superfluous things. Sometimes, it means cheerfully and magnanimously stepping on one's pride or saying 'No' to a whim. At times, it can even mean gladly bearing with discomfort or the lack of some indispensable item. To be poor is to make good use of the treasure of time. It is also seen in how one maintains household goods and appliances so that these may last, avoiding waste, and cutting down on useless expenses. Poverty may also call for "extending" the life of apparently worn-out or disposable things through recycling. In other words, a person who is poor in spirit knows how to be calm and cheerful when circumstances call for more self-abnegation and sacrifice.[22]

This is why a family with many children is the ideal setup for young people to learn to be generous and thoughtful. In such an environment, one cannot easily claim something to be "mine" or "yours." Clothing, the radio, the television set, and even the food and chocolates are "ours." What's more, everyone is equally responsible to make sure that these items should last. A big family is also the best place for the children to check each other's excesses. The younger siblings can easily protest the bullying of an older brother or make fun of the vanity or frivolity of an older sister. The older siblings, on the other hand, can help the younger ones study and get better grades and

[22] Cf. *Conversations*... nos. 110-111.

encourage them to temper whatever bad habits they may have.

Some Human Virtues

Human virtues are all those acquired habits that develop and define one's personality. They perfect a person, humanly speaking, and also prepare him to receive a life of grace and to engage in a personal relationship with God. The human virtues are the foundation on which the infused moral and theological virtues are built. When married couples work at becoming more mature persons, they acquire inner stability, prudence, discernment and sound judgment. In a word, they become more inclined to the good; they form their characters and become more and more masters of their lives. They acquire discipline, and are more inclined to be sincere, fair, and loyal to their commitments. It would be a mistake then to insist that one ought to develop the supernatural virtues when the basic human virtues are amiss. "Remember that even if your virtues seem saintly, they're worth nothing if they are not united to the ordinary Christian virtues. That would be like adorning yourself with splendid jewels over your underclothes."[23] In this sense, we can consider some human virtues that are indispensable to seeking sanctity in one's marriage and family life.

[23] *The Way* no. 409.

Spirit of sacrifice

This means knowing how to take any discomfort or annoyance with, as much as possible, a cheerful and good humored attitude. It is a normal thing to experience misunderstandings and difficult moments in one's marriage, which is why one has to be virtuous to take it all in stride. Only then shall peace reign in the home and only then shall God's presence be more readily felt. As a consequence, it will be easier to follow Christ more closely, that is, to abide in him and to live in his presence. He said it: *If any man would come after me, let him deny himself and take up his cross daily and follow me.*[24]

Whoever is burdened by sorrow and pain must remember that our Redeemer asks us to be patient in bearing our troubles and to offer them up to him for the salvation of souls and the forgiveness of sins. And when the burden is simply unbearable, he invites us: *Come to me, all who labor and are heavy laden, and I will give you rest. Take my yoke upon you, and learn from me; for I am gentle and lowly in heart, and you will find rest for your souls. For my yoke is easy, and my burden is light.*[25]

In a predominantly comfort-loving and hedonistic environment, it will be good to foster the spirit of sacrifice in the home so that everyone may learn to generously spend one's self for the good of others. A specific way to do this is to observe a schedule. Thus one can beat the natural tendency to be lazy and to procrastinate. Living a spirit of sacrifice in fulfilling

[24] Lk 9:23.
[25] Mt 11:28-30.

one's duties helps harmonize family obligations with work and social commitments, as well as with the practice of one's religion. Clearly, the spirit of sacrifice and penance does an immense good to the formation of one's character and that of the children.

"Penance means being very charitable at all times towards those around you, starting with the members of your own family. It is to be full of tenderness and kindness towards the suffering, the sick and the infirm. It is to give patient answers to people who are boring and annoying. It means interrupting our work or changing our plans, when circumstances makes this necessary, above all when the just and rightful needs of others are involved.

Penance consists in putting up good-humoredly with the thousand and one little pinpricks of each day; in not abandoning your job, although you have momentarily lost the enthusiasm with which you started it; in eating gladly whatever is served, without being fussy.

For parents and, in general, for those whose work involves supervision or teaching, penance is to correct whenever it is necessary. This should be done bearing in mind the type of fault committed and the situation of the person who needs to be so helped, not letting oneself be swayed by subjective viewpoints, which are often cowardly and sentimental.

A spirit of penance keeps us from becoming too attached to the vast imaginative blueprints we have made for our future projects, where we have already foreseen our master strokes and brilliant successes. What joy we give to God when we are happy to lay aside our third-rate painting efforts and let *him* put in the features and colors of his choice![26]

Industriousness

Time is short and on Judgment Day we shall be asked to render an account of how we have spent the time granted to us here on Earth. Those squandered hours will then echo the Gospel parable of the wasted talents. One then realizes that the atmosphere of hard work in the family is crucial to the smooth-running of the home and to the common welfare and spiritual good of the whole family. There are only so many hours to a day and there is much to be done: The children have to be cared for; one must attend to a job and to the domestic chores; besides, one needs to make sure that everyone gets the much-needed rest and recreation. Nevertheless rest does not mean doing nothing; it means a change of activity, doing some-thing that is easier and more enjoyable, though never useless or pointless.

There is a constant battle to be waged against laziness, comfort-seeking and the tendency to choose the easy-way-out. We have to learn how to fulfill our duties perfectly, putting our heart into what we are doing and paying attention to the details. This is the measure of our love for God and neighbor. A person who works well and who pays attention to the details is usually considered reliable and trustworthy. He can be entrusted with greater tasks. That is why the Lord loves a hard worker who not only lovingly

[26] St J. Escrivá, *Friends of God* no. 138.

finishes the tasks entrusted to him but who does so ever aware that he is working in God's presence.[27]

Order and punctuality

These virtues may look trivial but are not because, without them, life would be a complete mayhem. A person who is disorderly and unpunctual not only wastes precious time but is himself a liability at work and a nuisance to his co-workers. There is no real virtue without a sense of order, both in the material sphere (in one's home, desk and closet) and in one's thoughts and affections. The latter calls for a hierarchy of values that enables a person to give priority where priority is due. This leads him to make the most of his time, following a well thought-out daily schedule. The former, on the other hand, is just as important. As one wise and experienced priest remarked, he can tell the state of a person's soul by looking inside his closet. This idea makes us examine ourselves regarding the value we give to things. If we easily overlook the divine transcendence of being orderly in the use of our time and of material things, then how easy it is to neglect our spiritual life and our relationship with God.

The same holds true for punctuality, a virtue oftentimes afforded scant attention. Charity and good manners demand that we do not make people wait. People who habitually arrive late for appointments are probably unaware of the bother they cause; they do not

[27] *His master said to him, 'Well done, good and faithful servant; you have been faithful over a little, I will set you over much; enter into the joy of your master.'* (Mt 25:21).

realize the amount of patience they exact from those who are forced to put up with them. Tardiness reflects not only a disorderly life, but also a kind of rudeness, laziness and self-indulgence.

Order and punctuality therefore are two little virtues that mean so much to running a home well. And the home offers many opportunities to practice these virtues: serving the meals on time, having the laundry ready when people need them, returning items to their proper places, coming home on time and not allowing others to wait up. Such opportunities not only make a person better; they also teach and edify the others who see these virtues being lived.

Serenity and cheerfulness

These are fruits of the many other virtues that have been tackled. In hard times, a warm smile is most welcome. When unforeseen setbacks come around, cool heads and an optimistic attitude always come in handy. It is not easy to be calm and cheerful in the face of life's many trials and sorrows. Nevertheless, one must be determined to make the effort. We may not get any thanks for favors extended, much less comfort and consolation when we are down. It does not matter. A good Christian knows that he does everything for God who *loves a cheerful giver*.[28]

Many other virtues, human and supernatural, come into play when Christian life is lived to the fullest. All together the virtues brighten up family life. But we do not wish to stop here. All virtues must be diligently fostered, not only to make one's home a pleasant place

[28] 2 Cor 9:7.

to live in, but also, and more fundamentally, to ensure constant progress along the path of holiness.

THE SPIRITUAL LIFE OF THE FAMILY

"Husband and wife are called to sanctify their married life and to sanctify themselves in it. It would be a serious mistake if they were to exclude family life from their spiritual development. The marriage union, the care and education of children, the effort to provide for the needs of the family as well as for its security and development, the relationships with other persons who make up the community, all these are among the ordinary human situations that Christian couples are called upon to sanctify."[29]

God is never indifferent to the most commonplace events in a Christian home. That is why marriage and the family provide the ideal conditions and opportunities for parents and children to direct their lives to God. And if the family takes advantage of these opportunities, then the divine meaning they give to life should come out naturally and spontaneously. But this can happen only if the couple, first of all, will follow the will of God wholeheartedly. This entails cultivating the different virtues that comprise, as it were, the warp and woof of the spiritual struggle. These virtues lay the foundation for a deep and fruitful interior life that enables one to transform work into prayer and maintain a constant dialogue with our Father God.

[29] *Christ is Passing By* no. 23.

It is not easy to define what a specifically conjugal spirituality should be or to enumerate the means to live it. It is not easy because each person must follow his own path and come to terms with specific problems and concerns. One's spiritual path should therefore take these factors into account. Still, some general guidelines do exist.

In the first place, Christian spouses follow a spirituality that is eminently lay and secular. It would be wrong for them to adopt a spirituality proper to a convent or monastery. The laity, of which the couple forms part, have a special vocation within the Church— a vocation that entails a specific mission which is to sanctify the temporal realities that fall within their field of competence.[30] It is this condition that determines the spirituality proper to married couples. It does not invite them to withdraw from the world the way members of the religious orders do. Instead they are encouraged to devote themselves to placing Christ at the summit of all human activities—that is, on top of all their family, social, and professional duties. This is what is meant by a genuine lay spirituality. In the case of married couples, this means finding Christ in and through the fulfillment of their family duties; it means showing their love for God in the effort to face the difficulties of married life with a generous heart

[30] Vatican Council II clearly affirms it: "By reason of their special vocation, it belongs to the laity to seek the kingdom of God by engaging in temporal affairs and directing them according to God's will... It pertains to them in a special way to so illuminate and order all temporal things with which they are so closely associated that these may be effected and grow according to Christ and may be to the glory of the Creator and Redeemer." (Const. LG 31).

and a spirit of self-abnegation. Thus, for instance, a husband and wife who practice a string of daily religious devotions and who may even be active in parish work or in some Catholic group cannot claim to be faithful to their vocation if they neglect their responsibilities as spouses and parents. That is, if they show no affection for each other in the many details of mutual self-giving in married life, if they easily complain about the usual problems that arise from running a home, or if they never agree on how to bring up their children properly.

In the second place, conjugal spirituality calls for husband and wife to harmonize their religious devotions with family obligations and the family's daily schedule. The faithful fulfillment of these devotions should facilitate rather than hinder the fulfillment of their duties. This is how the spouses honor God and serve him in a fitting manner. One needs piety to make supernatural sense out of fulfilling one's family duties; however, a twisted understanding of piety would only get in the way of running a home well. Religious and family duties should be carried out with love and constancy. Pious practices ought to help the spouses fulfill their primary mission of giving themselves fully to each other and to their children. Religious devotions sanctify the family by giving spouses and children a complete perspective of what family life is about.

Unfortunately, some good willed souls suffer needlessly when they create conflicts between their devotions and their family responsibilities. This problem would not exist if they realize that holiness must pervade in every corner of a Christian home:

from the silent effort to get over a painful moment, to the raucous joy of a family gathering; from petty quarrels that end with amends, to small victories that call for a celebration; from the extra attention lavished on someone who needs it, to the effort to overcome one's selfishness. Everything can be turned into a loving prayer to the Lord.

Pious Practices

Are pious devotions necessary? How many should they be? Which are the more important ones?

There are no clear-cut formulas to this. Just as there are a million and one ways by which one can show his love for someone, a person is just as free to express his love for God. Of course, this is not a question of stuffing the day with devotions. Let us not lose sight of the goal—to permeate all our activities with the love of God. This is why we offer to God at each moment, especially during Holy Mass, whatever it is that pains or saddens us. This is why we trustingly abandon ourselves into his hands. And this is also why we put heart and soul into acquiring a virtue or into overcoming a defect. For love of God, we smile even if we are annoyed, hold our tongue and forgive a person who angers us, and put our time, talents and resourcefulness at the service of others. This is why families strive to make their house a home. Family prayer then is like a common supplication raised to the Father, through the Son and with the Holy Spirit.

"Family prayer has for its very own object family life itself, which in all its varying circumstances is seen as a call from God and lived as a filial response to his call. Joys and sorrows, hopes and disappointments, births and birthday celebrations, wedding anniversaries of the parents, departures, separations and homecomings, important and far-reaching decisions, the death of those who are dear, etc.—all of these mark God's loving intervention in the family's history. They should be seen as suitable moments for thanksgiving, for petition, for trusting abandonment of the family into the hands of their common Father in heaven."[31]

Does this mean then that devotional practices are superfluous? Far from it: they are indispensable. It would be wrong to think that one fulfills his duties merely by avoiding bad things. Only one thing sanctifies—the love of God—and to love God, one must deal with him, seek his company and be friends with him. Which is why Jesus Christ became man in the first place. *I have called you friends*.[32] The personal, frequent encounter with Jesus in the Blessed Sacrament and in Confession is of primary importance because there, he offers Love in a special way. Both sacraments bestow and increase grace without which we can never progress in the spiritual life. There is also the need to pray and to offer sacrifices, which spiritual writers call the prayer of the body, and have a special love for the Blessed Virgin Mary. Through all these, we assimilate grace into our life.

[31] *FC* 59.
[32] Jn 15:15.

The Sunday Precept

We also remember that, as creatures and children of God, Christians have the obligation to attend Holy Mass every Sunday (or the evening of the previous day). All Christian families ought to look forward to Sunday as an opportunity to attend Holy Mass together. And for a good reason. All that we receive everyday comes from the hands of God. We are constantly under his loving care, benefited by his abundant goodness, and forgiven by his unfailing mercy. Thus, Pope John Paul II asks, "How could we not come together every Sunday to thank him for his good gifts and to ask pardon for our faults, to listen to his Word, to celebrate his mysteries, and eat the Bread of children, the 'bread from heaven, the true bread' which the Father gives us (cf. Jn 6:32)? Do not despise the invitation on Sunday to celebrate the Eucharist together."[33]

Let us pause to reflect on the Pope's words. Christ, through the Church, offers all Catholics an opportunity to celebrate a most eminent feast. In the apostolic letter *Dies Domini*, the Pope once again encourages us to celebrate Sunday and to give it its full spiritual and human significance without diminishing it to a mere weekend break devoted to rest and leisure.

"Sunday is a day that is at the very heart of the Christian life. From the beginning of my Pontificate, I have not ceased to repeat: *Do not be afraid! Open, open wide the doors to Christ!* In the same way, today I would strongly urge everyone to rediscover Sunday: *Do not be afraid to give your time to Christ!* Yes, let us open our

[33] Address at El Tunal Park in Bogota (Colombia), August 3, 1986.

time to Christ, that he may cast light upon it and give it direction. He is the One who knows the secret of time and the secret of eternity, and he gives us "his day" as an ever-new gift of his love. The rediscovery of this day is a grace that we must implore, not only so that we may live the demands of faith to the full, but also so that we may respond concretely to the deepest human yearnings. Time given to Christ is never time lost, but is rather time gained, so that our relationships and indeed our whole life may become more profoundly human...In effect, Sunday is the day above all other days that summons Christians to remember the salvation which was given to them in Baptism and which has made them new in Christ... Sunday, the day of light, could also be called the day of 'fire,' in reference to the Holy Spirit. The light of Christ is intimately linked to the 'fire' of the Spirit, and the two images together reveal the meaning of the Christian Sunday...Given these different dimensions which set it apart, Sunday appears as the supreme day of faith...It is clear then why, even in our own difficult times, the identity of this day must be protected and above all must be lived in all its depth."[34]

In a very significant way the *Catechism of the Catholic Church* points out that "The Sunday celebration of the Lord's Day and his Eucharist is at the heart of the Church's life."[35] For there, in the celebration of the Eucharist on Sunday, Christians profess their faith in the Resurrection and gather to themselves the fruits and merits that Christ won for us on the Cross.

[34] John Paul II, *Dies Domini* 7, 25, 28, 29, 30.
[35] *CCC* 2177.

Sunday Mass then is a privileged time where God directly shows his favor upon man. There, from the altar, the Son offers an expiatory sacrifice to the Father. The Holy Mass is the center of a Christian's spiritual life because this is when he pays the four "debts" of prayer that all men owe God: adoration, reparation, petition and thanksgiving. And, for the same reason, "among the many activities of a parish, none is as vital or as community-forming as the Sunday celebration of the Lord's Day and his Eucharist."[36]

"For Christian families, the Sunday assembly is one of the most outstanding expressions of their identity and their 'ministry' as 'domestic churches,' when parents share with their children at the one Table of the Word and of the Bread of Life. We do well to recall in this regard that it is first of all the parents who must teach their children to participate in Sunday Mass…Thus the liturgical reading of the Word of God is not as much as a moment to meditate and to instruct as one of a *dialogue of God with his people* wherein what is proclaimed are the marvels of salvation and the invitation to renew our commitment to the Covenant. The people of God are invited to respond in this dialogue of love with acts of thanksgiving and praise but at the same confirming their faithfulness to the covenant and working at a continuous conversion."[37]

The Mass is therefore the most fitting place for the renewal of Christ's sacrifice. There, as the people of God gather around the Altar, Christ offers himself in an ascending movement to the Father and in a descending movement to the faithful. Thus "the Mass in

---

[36] *Dies Domini* 30.
[37] *Ibid*. 36 and 41.

fact truly makes present the sacrifice of the Cross. Under the species of bread and wine, upon which has been invoked the outpouring of the Spirit who works with absolutely unique power in the words of consecration, Christ offers Himself to the Father in the same act of sacrifice by which He offered Himself on the Cross."[38] And when the faithful unite their lives, their praise, their work, their suffering with Christ's offering on the Cross, theirs becomes a total offering and acquires a new value.[39]

In this sense as the celebration moves on from the reading of the Word to the breaking of the Bread, the Church encourages the faithful to receive communion when they take part in the Eucharist. However, this is on the condition that they are properly disposed to receive the Lord and, if they have committed a grave sin, to receive God's pardon first in the Sacrament of Reconciliation.[40] It is in this very spirit that St Paul wrote the Christian community of Corinth.[41] And to all who respond to the invitation to receive Eucharistic communion most especially during Holy Mass on Sundays and holy days, the Pope reiterates: "It is also important to be ever mindful that communion with

[38] *Ibid.*43.

[39] *Ibid.*

[40] *Ibid.* 44.

[41] *Whoever, therefore, eats the bread or drinks the cup of the Lord in an unworthy manner will be guilty of profaning the body and blood of the Lord. Let a man examine himself, and so eat of the bread and drink of the cup. For any one who eats and drinks without discerning the body eats and drinks judgment upon himself. That is why many of you are weak and ill, and some have died. But if we judged ourselves truly, we should not be judged. But when we are judged by the Lord, we are chastened so that we may not be condemned along with the world.* (1 Cor 11: 27-32).

Christ is deeply tied to communion with our brothers and sisters. The Sunday Eucharistic gathering is an experience of brotherhood, which the celebration should demonstrate clearly, while ever respecting the nature of the liturgical action."[42]

The Sunday precept has always been understood as a grave obligation.[43] This may be better understood if one considers the importance of Sundays to Christian life. Again, in the same exhortation, the Pope invokes the heroism of our Christian ancestors and of those in present times in many parts of the world where Christians continue to suffer for wanting to adhere to their faith. For many times, the environment is either indifferent or hostile to the Gospel, and believers who refuse to be enslaved by their surroundings rely precisely on the support of their brothers in the faith, the Christian community. When one comes down to think about it, one can conclude that it is indeed crucial to gather with other believers in the faith to celebrate the Lord's Paschal Sacrifice of the New Covenant. [44]

This is also why "pastors have the corresponding duty to offer to everyone the real possibility of fulfilling the precept. The provisions of Church law move in this direction as, for example, in the faculty granted to

[42] *Dies Domini* 44.

[43] "The Sunday Eucharist is the foundation and confirmation of all Christian practice. For this reason the faithful are obliged to participate in the Eucharist on days of obligation, unless excused for a serious reason (for example, illness, the care of infants) or dispensed by their own pastor. Those who deliberately fail in this obligation commit a grave sin." *CCC* 2181.

[44] Cf. *Dies Domini* 48.

priests, with the prior authorization of the diocesan Bishop, to celebrate more than one Mass on Sundays and holy days, the institution of evening Masses and the provision which allows the obligation to be fulfilled from Saturday evening onwards, starting at the time of First Vespers of Sunday. Given the nature of Sunday Mass and its importance in the lives of the faithful, it must be prepared with special care. In ways dictated by pastoral experience and local customs in keeping with liturgical norms, efforts must be made to ensure that the celebration has the festive character appropriate to the day commemorating the Lord's Resurrection. To this end, it is important to devote attention to the songs used by the assembly, since singing is a particularly apt way to express a joyful heart, accentuating the solemnity of the celebration and fostering the sense of a common faith and a shared love."[45]

"In fact, the Lord's Day is lived well if it is marked from beginning to end by grateful and active remembrance of God's saving work. This commits each of Christ's disciples to shape the other moments of the day, those outside the liturgical context: family life, social relationships, moments of relaxation in such a way that the peace and joy of the Risen Lord will emerge in the ordinary events of life. For example, the relaxed gathering of parents and children can be an opportunity not only to listen to one another but also to share a few formative and more reflective moments."[46]

In the same light, the authentic "celebration" of the Lord's day should bring about true human and spiritual growth. "Through the Sunday rest, daily

[45] *Ibid.* 50.
[46] *Ibid.* 52.

concerns and tasks can find their proper perspective: the material things about which we worry give way to spiritual values; in a moment of encounter and less pressured exchange, we see the true face of the people with whom we live. Even the beauties of nature, too often marred by the desire to exploit, which turns against man himself, can be rediscovered and enjoyed to the full."[47]

Another way to make Sundays more Christ-centered is to think about one's neighbor. Since the early Christian times, Sunday gatherings were also dedicated to sharing one's goods with the less fortunate brethren. Thus, "Sundays should also give the faithful an opportunity to devote themselves to works of mercy, charity and apostolate."[48] Christians cannot be satisfied keeping to themselves. "They look around to find people who may need their help. It may be that in their neighborhood or among those they know, there are sick people, elderly people, children or immigrants who precisely on Sundays feel more keenly their isolation, needs and suffering...Inviting to a meal people who are alone, visiting the sick, providing food for needy families, spending a few hours in voluntary work and acts of solidarity: these would certainly be ways of bringing into people's lives the love of Christ received at the Eucharistic table.[49] In this way the Sunday observance is not limited to the Eucharistic celebration; it also becomes a great school of virtues: of charity, justice and peace.[50]

[47] *Ibid*. 67.
[48] *Ibid*. 69.
[49] *Ibid*. 72.
[50] *Ibid*. 73.

OTHER PIOUS PRACTICES

There are many other Christian customs that the family can adopt in order to honor God. These include praying the Morning Offering; reading the Bible or a spiritual book for a few minutes; saying the Holy Rosary; praying three Hail Mary(s) before going to bed, beseeching Our Lady to *pray for us sinners, now and at the hour of our death;* and casting an affectionate glance at an image of Mary as one enters or leaves the house. There is also such a thing called personal meditation wherein one engages in a loving, friendly and personal dialogue with Jesus. The day must not end without briefly examining one's conscience, thanking God for the good things done, asking him pardon for the bad, and asking help for the next day's battle.

There is no reason why religious devotions should hinder one from paying full attention to work and family obligations. On the contrary, they should lead us to discover God in those very realities and to show our confidence in him. Pious practices should in fact spring naturally and spontaneously from a Christian parent's heart because it is the result of one's inner dispositions; and parents ought to be living models of Christian piety to their children.

"Experience show in all Christian environments what good effects come from this natural and supernatural introduction to the life of piety given in the warmth of the home. Children learn to place God first and foremost in their affections. They learn to see God as their Father and Mary as their Mother and learn to pray following their parents' example. In this way, one can easily see what a wonderful apostolate parents have and how it is their duty to live a fully Christian life of prayer, so they can communicate their love of God to their children, which is something more than just teaching them.

How can they go about this? They have excellent means in the few, short, daily religious practices that have always been lived in Christian families and which I think are marvelous: grace at meals, morning and night prayers, the family rosary (even though nowadays some people criticize this devotion to our Lady). Customs vary from place to place, but I think one should always encourage some acts of piety which the family can do together in a simple and natural fashion.

This is the way to ensure that God is not regarded as a stranger whom we go to see in church once a week on Sunday. He will be seen and treated as he really is, not only in church but also at home, because our Lord has told us, "Where two or three are gathered in My name, I am there in the midst of them (Mt 18:20).'

I still pray aloud the bedside prayers I learned as a child from my mother's lips and I say so with the pride and gratitude of a son. They bring me closer to God and make me feel the love with which I learned to take my first steps as a Christian. And as I offer to God the day that is beginning or thank him for the day that is drawing to a close, I ask him to increase in heaven the happiness of those whom I especially love and to unite us there forever."[51]

[51] *Conversations...* no. 103.

UNITY IN THE SPIRITUAL LIFE OF MARRIED COUPLES

Married couples do well in working at deeper unity in their spiritual life, which is the ultimate kind of oneness that spouses can achieve. Unity in spiritual life affects the deepest recesses of the soul and thus becomes the spouses' reference point for the basic and crucial decisions that they must take in life. The consequence of spiritual unity is a great sense of peace that the Holy Spirit grants those souls who desire to be one in their faith and in their love for God.

Nevertheless, couples need not share everything in the way they live their life in the spirit. For God grants each person specific graces to which one must correspond in all freedom and responsibility. For example, the husband is not obliged to practice the devotions of his wife. Neither one should set one's self as a model for the other because Jesus Christ is the only model for all. With this in mind, spouses can acquire deeper spiritual union in a way that they walk toward the same goal. They may probably follow the same path. Even so, spouses who happen to follow the same spiritual path must respect one another and allow the devotions or acts of piety that he or she prefers to do.

Married couples can help each other improve their spiritual life by not opposing or putting obstacles to one's choice of spiritual formation and guidance. Spouses need not have the same manner of expressing piety; neither do they have to be part of the same religious organization. Much less should they try to be a self-proclaimed spiritual director of the other. In the sphere of the interior life, spouses must allow their partner to freely follow the dictates of his or her conscience. It may take just one sarcastic remark or a bad joke to inhibit the spiritual freedom of the other. A husband cannot impose his manner of praying on his wife; a wife cannot demand that her husband practice her religious devotions.

It is enough that they respect and understand each other and thus each one, side by side, will discover God and seek the sanctity to which all the children of God are called. To impose uniformity on the way a married couple relates to God tells of a warped sense of spirituality. One therefore must not feel hurt that his or her spouse spends more time in prayer or receives Holy Communion more frequently than he or she does. Piety is built on a soul's personal relationship with God. What the Holy Spirit suggests to one is not necessarily the same as what he would tell the other. It would be a big mistake to think that the sacred bond of marriage should extend to the spirituality of each spouse.

For the same reason, the spouse who is more spiritually "advanced" should never chide the other for "lagging behind." A more positive approach to this, as we have seen earlier, is for each one to facilitate the spiritual progress of the other, but always discreetly and with a lot of tact. The partner who, for one reason or another, is less inclined to a life of piety or is perhaps more reserved and uncommunicative about it, has the right to discover the spiritual life on his or her initiative and to pursue it at his or her pace. The good example of the more pious spouse accomplishes much more than nagging and badgering.

It is easy to see how freedom is basic to the growth of interior life. A person's effort to encounter God should spring from the innermost recesses of the heart—fruit of a free and conscientious decision. Which means that one can never compel the other to take his or her spiritual life seriously; a wise and loving spouse can only extend a helping hand. If God shows utmost respect for the freedom of his creatures, then a husband or wife cannot say that he or she is right to impose on his or her partner what the Holy Spirit only counsels or suggests.

These are the general guidelines to a spirituality suitable to married couples. Christian couples who seek sanctity in and through their married life should strive to reflect the light of Christ in their homes. The bright and cheerful atmosphere that they radiate must be fruit of the harmony among the members of the family. The harmony between parents is passed on to the children and the domestic staff who, in turn, pass this on to their wider circle of friends and acquaintances. From this perspective, we can say that a truly Christian family is a replica of the mystery of the Church founded by God to act as a beacon to the world.

THE FAMILY APOSTOLATE

Married couples who cultivate the Christian virtues and who strive for holiness will find themselves becoming more and more identified with Christ and his work of redemption. This happens as they give constant and good example to everyone around them, within the home and outside of it. Christian spouses bring Christ everywhere they go by "contaminating" others with their cheerfulness and serenity. This is apostolate in the true sense of the word, the generous effort to bear witness to the Gospel through one's life and word, ever-respectful of the freedom of others.

The merits of Christ's Redemption are infinite. Nevertheless, our Lord wishes the baptized faithful to collaborate with his saving mission. In other words, he calls them to co-redeem with him. Through the work of the Holy Spirit, he enlivens them with grace, encourages them along the road to holiness, and entrusts them to help others be holy. This is why a Christian who is coherent with his faith sees life in a new perspective. He is aware that his reason for being is to collaborate with God in an undertaking that is at once human and divine. He greatly longs to fill the world with God's loving presence. This is the wonderful apostolic panorama that opens up to the Christian who yearns to bring his relatives, friends and colleagues closer to Christ. He is convinced that this pressing concern is not futile and he knows that he is not alone in fighting the baneful effects of his weaknesses and those of others. At all times he feels the assurance of God-made-man and strives to bring others to share the experience of having Jesus our Lord so close as to call us his friends. To be a friend of God is an honorable title indeed—and a weighty commitment: *This is my commandment, that you love one another as I have loved you. Greater love has no man than this, that a man lay down his life for his friends. You are my friends if you do what I command you.*[52] To give one's life means

---

[52] Jn 15:12-14.

to deny one's self in order to devote one's energies to the service of others; it means a readiness to undergo any sacrifice, big or small, so that others may be happy. It means being free from any personal complications in order to help others carry their burdens. *Bear one another's burdens, and so fulfill the law of Christ.*[53] *For he who loves his neighbor has fulfilled the law... Therefore love is the fulfilling of the law.*[54]

In this world wallowing in material misery, widespread ignorance and a glaring loss of faith, a Christian who wants to be consequent with his beliefs must see in all this a call to be responsible, charitable and just toward his neighbors. "Our neighbor's problems must be our problems. Christian fraternity should be something very deep in the soul so that we are indifferent to no one."[55] However there exists a yet more serious and widespread evil. This is the sad state of morality that marks our times. Many may not be alarmed by it but the consequences are deeply felt and far reaching. The streets, movie houses and the mass media all reflect this condition. It is the root of the alarming disregard for the dignity of human life. One can think not only of those horrible crimes and unjust wars that men perpetrate against their fellows but also of the systematic killing of innocent lives in the wombs of their mothers. This sad state of morality is also seen in the proliferation of drugs, the degradation of women, the commercialization of sex, and the blatant loss of modesty in dress and behavior.

[53] Gal 6:2.
[54] Rom 13:8, 10.
[55] *Christ is Passing By* no. 145.

A progressive de-Christianization of society is taking place and its fatal seeds have taken root even in the convents and seminaries. The extent to which the Faith is being undermined in some places can be gauged by the twisted interpretations of the Gospel from the pulpit: attacks against the Real Presence of Jesus Christ in the Holy Eucharist, and against the sacraments, priestly celibacy and the indissolubility of marriage. The so-called culture of death directly opposes the Gospel's message of life and converts the maternal womb into a death chamber. An urgent call from on high is heard amidst all these evils. Christians are called to work together at spreading the Kingdom. Many respond by totally surrendering themselves to God in a life of apostolic celibacy; others follow a priestly or a religious vocation. But many more are needed. *The harvest is plentiful but the laborers are few.*[56]

The great majority still refuses to get involved. "What can we do? We are in no position to help. Not with so many pressing family and professional obligations. Are we to neglect all this to fulfill the commandment of charity?" Certainly not. The Church asks her children to work for the Christian transformation of society from the very place they find themselves, not abandoning their temporal commitments. From this vantage point, they will spread the Gospel message to others. Just think: If everyone sweeps his part of the sidewalk, then the whole neighborhood would be clean. One does not have to do strange or spectacular feats to serve God and neighbor. One can place Christ at the heart of all human activities in a

[56] Lk 10:2.

very natural way, living in the middle of the world, devoted to one's professional work and to the care of one's family, sharing the noble interests of men, and respecting the rightful freedom of every man.[57]

It would then be sheer folly to ask Christians to abandon their family and job and launch out to become an apostle. On the other hand, if each one were to fulfill the duties of his state in life to his best ability, if everyone were to live his vocation to the full, then society as a whole would benefit more than it ever would from any other plan.

"But let's not think of ourselves. Expand your heart until it takes in all of mankind. Above all, think of those near you—relatives, friends, colleagues—and see how you can get them to appreciate a deeper friendship with our Lord...A Christian cannot be selfish. If he were, he would betray his vocation. Far from Christ are those content with keeping their soul in peace—and a false peace at that—while ignoring the good of others.

If we have accepted the authentic meaning of human life, which is revealed to us in faith, we cannot remain peacefully on the sidelines. If in a practical and concrete way we aren't drawing others to God, we can't be at all satisfied with our behavior."[58]

A Christian apostle therefore is one who fulfills his professional, family, and social obligations well because in doing so he renders a direct service to the Church and to one's neighbor. All human endeavors can be turned into a means to improve society. What does this entail in family life? We have already seen

[57] Cf. *Christ is Passing By* no. 148.
[58] *Ibid*. 175.

that all the virtues can be practiced in the home. Family relationships already offer many opportunities to bring souls to God. Thus when faith inspires and transforms a Christian family, the home naturally becomes an excellent training ground for Christian apostles.

Take this wonderful example of a mother of three. All her children have grown and for several years now she has been giving her three sons and their girl-friends weekly lessons in the catechism of the Catholic Church. Her audience, all college students, look forward to these sessions and even go out of their way to attend the classes that they would miss. The secret? This lady not only prepares her lessons well so that she can explain things clearly while stimulating the minds of her young listeners; she also makes sure that her classes are marked by a good sense of humor, graciousness and a lot of youthful flair. Proof that a mother can indeed bridge the generation gap. Think, too, of this family that gladly takes a whole afternoon off to drive to the next city where the children can receive the religious instruction that their own school does not offer.

Parents are certainly the primary educators of their children. Through their word and example, they train their sons and daughters to know and to practice the human and the supernatural virtues, and to know and serve God and neighbor. The home is the best place to instill children's minds with the need to be concerned about the welfare of others. Values and positive ideas are more easily inculcated in a big family, where selfishness is practically out of the question and where the eyes and hearts of the young are slowly opened to noble ideals. They learn to be amiable with others, regardless of color, economic status or religion. They become sensitive to the sufferings of others and appreciate the need to be in solidarity with all men, a value that is sorely absent in these times.

On the other hand, think of the harm that flippant behavior or frivolous conversation can do to a child. This may probably come in gossip about some celebrity couple who recently divorced and are now dating different partners or what values can a father inculcate in his son who sees him raving about the victory of his favorite basketball team but who is indifferent to news about the latest Nobel Peace Price winner or the historic visit of a world leader to one's country? What can a mother teach her daughter who sees her quite informed about the shady past of a beauty title holder, but who has nothing substantial to say about a war or a natural calamity that left 10,000 dead or homeless? Can you teach your child to take intelligent stock of things and events if it seems all the same to you whether it is a laboratory rat or a person that just died? A parent's joy, sadness or apathy reflects the hierarchy of values that they are transmitting to their children. Parents certainly form their children who observe the way they read the papers or watch television. A great part of a child's education depends on the kind of books and magazines that enter the home. Clearly, education is integral to doing apostolate in the home.

THE FAMILY IN SOCIETY

The family as part of a larger society is entrusted with a four-fold mission:
- to form a community of persons
- to serve life
- to participate in the development of society
- to participate in the life and mission of the Church

The family is the original cell of society and is therefore the foundation of all societies, or the germ of a new one. It is within a community that a person, from infancy, learns the moral values and the duty to honor God and to make good use of one's freedom. Life in the family is an initiation to life in society at large. This is why homes ought to foster in the children, from their earliest years, a sense of concern and responsibility for all the members of the family—from the infants to the elderly, from the sick to the poor and the disabled.

The fourth commandment sheds light on the other relationships that one forms within a society. It is easy to grasp how siblings are related, since they come from the same parents; and cousins, as they have the same grandparents. On a wider scale, citizens of the same country are related to each other because they share the same race, geographical space, history and cultural heritage. All the baptized Catholic faithful are related because they are one in the same faith and are children of one Mother, the Catholic Church. Finally, all human beings are children of the same Father, God. From these ideas we can conclude that every relationship one gets into is *personal* in nature.

And, within a family, one's neighbor is not just "any one" but "someone" who, because of his roots and bloodline, is one's closest neighbor and so deserves special attention and respect.[59]

This also means that the well-being of a person, of a society and, in fact, of all men, is closely related to the well-being of the family. For the family is a gift to society and, consequently, demands proper recognition and adequate support. Likewise, the family demands that all homes take on their mission to work hand-in-hand for a better world. Far from enclosing itself in an ivory tower, the Christian family is called to open itself to other families and to society and assume its designated role in society.[60]

One therefore realizes that the observance and exercise of family values is not confined, so to speak, to one's backyard. Families have a specific duty to work together in the interest of man and to re-humanize mankind. As a structure, the family is the place where the private and public spheres of human life meet and, as such, it cannot withdraw to its intimate confines out of a false and deformed sense of privacy. Rather, the family is called to get involved in and reckon with the problems of society. In the advanced, industrialized societies, the involvement of the family in public life is more pronounced—a condition that is practically *sine qua non* in the right fulfillment of its mission to educate.[61]

[59] Cf. *CCC* 2207-2208, 2213.

[60] Cf. Alfonso Cardinal Lopez Trujillo, Theological-Pastoral Congress *The Family: Gift and Commitment, Hope of Humanity*, Rio de Janeiro, October 1-3, 1997.

[61] G. Campanini, *Family* in *New Dictionary of Moral Theology*, San Paolo, Milan, 1990, 411.

John Paul II highlights the importance of the family as a "primordial" and, in a sense, a "sovereign" society. The sovereignty of the family as a society lies in its being a social individual whose "specific and spiritual" sovereignty and rights are strongly bound to man's basic rights. Through the family, God's plans for man are carried out. The family is a necessary good for society and when it is not respected and helped but hindered and downgraded, man is left in a disastrous and immense vacuum. Thus the Pope says, "The family is at the heart of all these problems and tasks. To relegate it to a subordinate or secondary role, excluding it from its rightful position in society, would be to inflict grave harm on the authentic growth of society as a whole."[62]

With this idea, another form of apostolate emerges from within the family itself. St Paul even recommends it in his letter to the Romans: *practice hospitality*.[63] A home that breathes of affection, openness and friendship can well be the smiling face of the Church. The apostolate of hospitality can never be substituted, and Christians ought to be generous in carrying it out. The Christian family is also called to be a witness to disinterested self-giving when it comes to involvement in social problems. Such concern may be seen in a sincere interest to help the poor and the needy in body and in spirit, the outcasts of society, the elderly, the sick, the drug addicts, and the homeless.[64]

---

[62] John Paul II, *Letter to Families*, no. 17.
[63] Rom 12:13.
[64] Cf. *FC* 47.

Again, the documents of the Second Vatican Council point out other areas where married Catholics can help the Church build and sanctify society on a firm Christian foundation. Chapter 3 of the Decree on the apostolate of the laymen, for instance, speaks of the role of married couples in defending the sanctity and indissolubility of the marital bond. Obviously, without having to say much, the very life of Christian spouses stands as a witness to being faithful to God and His Law. By contrast, we know of the scandal caused by supposedly pious people—not to mention leaders of associations of Christian faithful—who behave like pagans in their daily domestic life.

Married couples also engage in an active Christian apostolate when they participate in social gatherings and in their involvement with numerous civil groups and institutions. When they meet with other parents in such settings, they vigorously affirm their right and duty to educate their children in freedom, as well as their right to choose what they believe to be the best school for their children. They likewise uphold the family's dignity and legitimate independence to choose the way they wish to run their home. And, in accordance with the dictates of conscience and without being pressured by the government or the mass media, married couples are free to decide on the number of children that they can raise. This is why we call upon the civil authorities to defend the family as a civil entity. Civil law should provide opportunities for families to enjoy a decent and dignified home, income-generating opportunities, social security, family-friendly taxation, and other means of government support.

In the same vein, married couples have the duty as apostles to demand from the Church the appropriate Christian formation for themselves and for their entire household. They have the right to require from their pastors a simple but clear explanation of the Gospel, without resorting to all-too human considerations or trendy interpretations that contradict the teaching authority of the Church. They must also learn to demand for everything they need to live their faith well—that is, the grace of the sacraments and the best possible spiritual guidance and instruction.

"The right to hear the word of God and the right to the sacraments are perhaps the most fundamental and elementary of all. They are the condition *sine qua non*, the absolutely necessary means, to exercise the unrenounceable (*sic*) and primary right to belong to the Church and to participate in the achievement of its common goals...The first and most fundamental duty of the Hierarchy and the first and most fundamental right of the faithful is to receive the Word of God and the Sacraments."[65]

We can list many other ways by which the family can serve society. When a home takes in an abandoned child and gives it love and the proper upbringing, the family is already working at bringing one more soul to God. Similarly, Christian parents work as apostles in the educational setting when they take time out from their home and work duties to collaborate in improving the curriculum and the management of a school. They do apostolate, too, through their active participation in parent counseling services or when they offer financial

[65] Bishop A. del Portillo, *Faithful and Laity in the Church*, 42.

support to associations whose objective is to help the family. Married couples can also work with young people, "supporting adolescents with [their] advice and help, assisting engaged couples to make a better preparation for marriage, taking a share in teaching catechism, supporting married people and families in a material or moral crisis, and, in the case of the aged, not only providing them with what is indispensable, but also procuring for them a fair share of the fruits of economic progress."[66]

Still, the more important kind of apostolate that Christian couples can carry out nowadays is their silent and honest example of virtue that constantly tells of the faith they profess. Faith lived and which radiates from a Christian home is the best testimony. A couple who have remained faithful to each other despite the most severe trials and difficulties greatly encourage many married people who may be overwhelmed by a pagan environment that scorns conjugal fidelity. Likewise, a Christian couple's generous collaboration with God to bring forth new lives into the world serves as a lesson to others who put up many obstacles and excuses in this regard. The excellent Christian upbringing of children, fruit of their parents' persevering and untiring attention, offers hope and inspiration to many parents who are probably baffled and at a loss over their own children's wayward ways.

The silent testimony to a truly Christian life lends considerable weight and efficacy to the advice of couples who, in an informal setting as well as in formal lectures and conferences, speak of the Christian

---

[66] Vatican Council II, Decree *Apostolicam actuositatem* 11.

doctrine regarding the family. As the Second Vatican Council states:

"The laity become powerful heralds of the faith in things to be hoped for (cf. Heb 11:1) if they join unhesitating profession of faith to the life of faith. This evangelization, that is, the proclamation of Christ by word and the testimony of life, acquires a specific property and peculiar efficacy because it is accomplished in the ordinary circumstances of the world."[67]

The same Council stresses the need to unite the apostolate of giving example with the apostolate of the word. It exhorts Catholics to use every opportunity to speak to others about the faith they profess. "This witness of life, however, is not the sole element in the apostolate; the true apostle is on the lookout for occasions of announcing Christ by word, either to unbelievers to draw them towards the faith, or to the faithful to instruct them, strengthen them, incite them to a more fervent life; *for Christ's love urges on* (2 Cor 5:14), and in the hearts of all should the Apostle's words find echo: *Woe to me if I do not preach the Gospel* (1 Cor 9:16).[68]

Even in their normal conversations at work or in social gatherings, Christian couples can well and very naturally clear up doubts regarding the moral law and family life and offer correct ideas about marriage and the upbringing of children. They should feel in a special way "the noble obligation of working to bring all men throughout the whole world to hear and accept the divine message of salvation."[69] The Second

---

[67] *LG* 35.
[68] *AA* 6.
[69] *Ibid.* 3.

Vatican Council in fact urges all the lay faithful to fulfill the mission that is rightly theirs: to bring Christ to all temporal activities. "The Council earnestly exhorts the laity to take a more active part, each according to his talents and knowledge and in fidelity to the mind of the Church, in the explanation and defense of Christian principles and in the correct application of them to the problems of our times."[70]

In this case, even those moments of leisure are opportunities for Christian couples to imbue a Christian sense in the way people spend their rest and recreation. Efforts in this regard "remedy the institutions and conditions of the world when they are an inducement to sin."[71] By the way they speak and behave, Christian couples must work for a healthy moral environment in the field of entertainment because it is not easy to form Christian homes when young people are easy prey to libertine influences. It is the job of Christian parents to drown evil with an abundance of good. They render invaluable service to society when they strive to foster clean and intelligent means of entertainment which are as far removed from prudishness as they are from frivolity and worldliness.

To summarize, the foremost task of Christian parents is to form children who can be real apostles. Start them off young. From their earliest years, children should be made to understand the value of serving others and of helping their friends seek the only true good, which is God. They ought to discover that doing apostolate is the greatest sign of charity and the best way to live the demands of the First Commandment.

[70] *Ibid.* 6.
[71] *LG* 36.

And they should try to share their parents' concern to build the edifice of the Christian life on solid ground.

There are many ways to go about this formative task and much will depend on the commitment and zeal of the parents themselves. If the couple is genuinely apostolic in their concerns, they will know how to use every opportunity to transmit the same concern to their children. Their example is the best teacher. The parents' zeal to give glory to God and to save souls is like a burning ember that will warm the hearts of the children and inflame in them a love for their neighbor and the desire to bring their friends to the warmth and love of Christ.[72] In this way, the children will want to be daring, charitable, understanding, and cheerful. They will want to work at being of service to others and to grow in the spirit of penance and self-renunciation. They will nurture the supernatural virtues of faith, hope and charity. In a word, they will acquire a host of virtues that will make them better instruments in God's hands for the redemption of men.

---

[72] "Do you see your brother in danger? Draw him aside and point the danger out to him in earnest. This must be your manner of behavior if you have zeal for God's house. Draw everyone you can to God through your affection and do not desist from this endeavor...Let me give you a word of advice— or better, let him who dwells within you to give it; after all, it is he who speaks, albeit through me: if God comes to you and enters your heart with his words, rest not until you have won other souls for Christ for this is a true sign that Christ has won you for himself." (St Augustine, *In Iohann. Ev. tract.*, 10, 9).

Epilogue

The Family: Hope of Humanity[1]

We conclude our book on marriage as a divine vocation on earth with the consideration that marriage is a process whereby two people in love unite and become one flesh and one spirit. Thus this seemingly human commitment between husband and wife becomes their road to salvation and gateway to eternal life. Their complete unity in body and spirit are assumed into an ultimate union with God.

"We have tried to mention and comment on some of the characteristics of a family that reflects the light of Christ… a home full of light and cheerfulness. The unity between parents is transmitted to their children, to the whole family, and to everyone who is involved in their life. In this way, every truly Christian family reproduces in some way the mystery of the Church, chosen by God, and sent to be the guide of the world."[2]

[1] We end with ideas culled from Alfonso Card. López Trujillo's words in the family congress *Gift and Commitment, Hope of Humanity,* Rio de Janeiro, October 1997.

[2] *Christ is Passing By* no. 30.

This thought should bring hope to many hearts so that married couples everywhere may look forward with confidence to a new century and squarely face the obstacles posed by a handful who raise a hostile clamor against the institution of marriage. God, the Lord of the future, has placed this period in our hands so that we may take full, personal responsibility for it. Christian spouses therefore cannot be deserters in such a decisive battle.

As we have seen throughout this work, the family is most intimately linked with the divine plan of the Incarnation. For did not the Son of God step into human history through the family of Nazareth? In Nazareth, *the Word became flesh*[3] and from that humble village proceeds the sublime image of the Holy Family, the model for all families and an inexhaustible source of spiritual energy on account of the merits of the Resurrected One.[4] As the Old Testament puts it, God pitched his tent among men; and Jesus Christ did so in this particular home, where he received his first lessons in life under the close supervision of his earthly parents.

Now, as we have crossed the threshold of the third millenium, amidst war, turbulence and anxiety, the Lord continues to go out of his way to have a personal encounter with all families. He wants to enlighten them, strengthen them, and redeem them with his Love. He walks by their side, striking tender conversation with them, a dialogue filled with concern and solicitude. This, one must discover through prayer and the eyes of faith because the pilgrimage is arduous: one

[3] Jn 1:14.
[4] Cf. John Paul II, Apostolic letter *Tertio millennio adveniente* 1.

witnesses and experiences the bitterness of defeat, battles lost, and the break up of many-a-home. Still, like those pilgrims headed for Emaus, we are in close touch with the Savior and, thanks to this fact, hope is born from an apparently lost cause.

Human love that is redeemed by God is an awesome reserve of the spiritual energy needed to face life's challenges and to take on the duties that the Lord requires of those to whom he has entrusted the family. Without this inner strength, man and the Church herself would be condemned to failure. Pope John Paul II stresses that the future of man takes place within the family. One ought to reflect upon this idea many times and discover the vast field of opportunities, realizing that the future of the family depends on how it accepts the invitation of the Lord of history. For, in great many ways, the family is the architect of its own destiny.

To hope in the Lord is crucial to the right fulfillment of this task. Hope is a virtue inscribed in the human heart and constitutes the core of one's self. It is proper to man to hope and to take heart. Christian hope and optimism is a "reaching out" to God, but without it degenerating into irresponsibility or presumption. In this crucial moment of our history, one must revive the conditions to hope. Genuine hope, just like Truth and authentic Charity, is never deceptive or delusional because it is not a human invention, but rather a solid, necessary and absolute trust in God. Christ's Cross is not a symbol of defeat because he resurrected soon after and then triumphantly ascended into Heaven. Christ's victory is ours. This is why we nurture hope and trust in the very source of love. In Kenya, they say that it is easier to climb a mountain when a friend awaits you at the top. In the same light, our hope that the family will endure as a solid support for mankind in this new century is founded on God's promises.

"The virtue of hope responds to the aspirations to happiness which God has placed in the heart of every man; it takes up the hopes that inspire men's activities and purifies them so as to order them to the Kingdom of heaven; it keeps man from discouragement; it sustains him during times of abandonment; it opens up his heart in expectation of eternal beatitude. Buoyed up by hope, he is preserved from selfishness and led to the happiness that flows from charity."[5]

Hope makes us look up to Heaven as our anchor and support because we know that the Lord has gone there ahead of us. But how can we hope when current trends of thought seem to breed more doubt than certainty? It is true that many families suffer from evident symptoms of decay. The media and certain international forums demonstrate the serious fissures in the family structure and even have a term for it: the family at a crossroad.

Nevertheless, such claims can only be taken as unfair generalizations that are alarming indeed, but specific to certain places. For even in countries that are hardest hit by the systematic destruction of the family, one can wonder at the counter-wave of opinions and movements that have gained ground even in the political arena, lobbying for changes and a "new deal." In not a few places, State policies have taken on a new attitude toward the family. It is not true that the prevailing anti-family mindset has eclipsed the home. If the Creator has expressly wished that this institution

5 *CCC* 1818.

should endure, then it is possible that deep in the hearts of nations and people lies the desire to seek the necessary good of married couples, children and society.

The family is the teacher of nations. It has and shall continue to be the fountainhead of culture and humanity. Moreover, the role of the home in the formation of a person can never be replaced. A child is always synonymous with hope; this is what makes a child important, even powerful. Concern for the child as such makes the family indispensable. Many couples ensnared by selfishness break free because of the desire to serve the child. The child, fruit of married love, teaches something very important to the very people who helped God bring him to life. The child prevents his parents from drowning in their own problems. The child moves them to live less for themselves and to think about consolidating hearth and home.[6]

[6] An international family congress which was sponsored by the United Nations and held in Malta in November 1993 had as a main speaker French sociologist L. Rousell. This gentleman offered a gloomy forecast about the future of the family. He declared that hope was dead. In an interview with him at the end of the session, I dared to ask him if there was some slim chance to "hope against hope" (as Abraham did), because, if what he proposed was true, then all of humanity is headed for a bottomless pit. Rousell thought for a moment and then offered me his book, which I had already read up with great interest. Then, he replied, "I see a light at the end of the tunnel. And that light is the child." The child is the light and the cure, even if many still do not see it as such. And Cardinal Alfonso López Trujillo added, "Allow me an analogy. We at the Pontifical Council for the Family received a gift from a famous Spanish sculptor named Luis Antonio Sanguino. It is called *Sanctuarium vitae*, a wonderful sculpture that is like a hymn to

To end, we invoke the protection of the Holy Family of Nazareth, the model of all Christian families. Jesus, Mary, and Joseph spent a life of obscurity in a small village of Palestine. These were years tested by poverty, persecution and exile, but which never lacked warmth, mutual love and affection. The Holy Family never fails to help Christian families, and all families the world over, to faithfully fulfill their daily obligations, cheerful amidst the trials of life and ever generous in helping and serving others.

Together with Pope John Paul II we pray:

May St Joseph—a 'just man,' a tireless worker, the upright guardian of those entrusted to his care—always guard, protect and enlighten families.

May the Virgin Mary, who is the Mother of the Church, also be the Mother of "the Church of the home." Thanks to her motherly aid, may each Christian family really become a 'little Church' in which the mystery of the Church of Christ is mirrored and given new life.

---

life. It depicts Christ, with his Divine and workman's hands pierced by nails, forming a crib of sorts. From it, life emerges as it would from the luminous womb of a woman—a mother. The unborn child then grows like a tree that branches out into a huge family made up of boys and girls of all races. These children lift their smiling faces and arms to heaven as though in triumph. I see the light that illuminates the womb as the love of husband and wife, of families, of the world. I believe that this work of art is a poetic and yet very realistic depiction of the "light at the end of tunnel." It is the light that the One from Nazareth and Bethlehem casts upon all men who are born into this world (Cf. Jn 1:9)."

May Christ the Lord, the Universal King, the King of Families, be present in every Christian home as He was at Cana, bestowing light, joy, serenity and strength. We entrust each family to Jesus, Mary and Joseph.[7]

---

[7] Cf. *FC* 86.

Bibliography

1) Saint Josemaría Escrivá
    The Way. Sinag-tala Publishers, 1998
    Friends of God. Sinag-tala Publishers, 1989
    Christ is Passing By. Sinag-tala Publishers, 1973
    Conversations with Monsignor Escrivá, 1970
2) Decree *Apostolicam actuositatem*. Vatican Council II
3) Documents of the Magisterium
    Catechism of the Catholic Church, 1992
    Code of Canon Law
4) Pastoral Constitution *Gaudium et spes*,
    Vatican Council II
5) Pope John Paul II
    Apostolic Exhortation *Familiaris consortio*,
        November 22, 1981
    Apostolic Letter *Dies Domini*, May 31, 1998
    Apostolic Letter *Tertio millenio adveniente*,
        November 10, 1994
    Encyclical *Evangelium vitae*, March 25, 1995
    Encyclical *Centesimus annus*, May 1, 1991
    Encyclical *Redemptor hominis*, March 4, 1979
    Letter to Families, February 2, 1994
    Love and Responsibility, 15th Edition
    Post-synodal apostolic exhortation
        Ecclesia in America, Mexico. January 22, 1999
6) Pope Paul VI
    Encyclical *Humanae vitae*, July 23, 1968

Index

Abbreviations

The following are abbreviations cited in the text:

AA	*APOSTOLICAM Actuositatem*
CCC	*Catechism of the Catholic Church*
FC	*FAMILIARIS Consortio*
GS	*GAUDIUM et Spes*
HV	*HUMANAE Vitae*
LG	*LUMEN Gentium*